# Costly Reflections in a Midas Mirror

# Costly Reflections in a Midas Mirror

## Fourth Edition

D. Larry Crumbley

Donald L. Ariail

Jeanne David

Veronica Paz

CAROLINA ACADEMIC PRESS

Durham, North Carolina

Library of Congress Cataloging-in-Publication Data
Names: Crumbley, D. Larry, author. | Ariail, Donald L., author. | David,
Jeanne, author.
Title: Costly reflections in a Midas mirror / D. Larry Crumbley, Donald L.
Ariail, Jeanne David, Veronica Paz.
Description: Fourth Edition. | Durham, N.C. : Carolina Academic Press, [2018]
| Revised edition of Costly reflections in a Midas mirror, c2011.
Identifiers: LCCN 2018038386 | ISBN 9781531012540 (alk. paper)
Subjects: LCSH: Cost accounting--Case studies. | Managerial accounting--
Case studies.
Classification: LCC HF5686.C8 C6995 2018 | DDC 657/.42--dc23
LC record available at https://lccn.loc.gov/2018038386
    e-ISBN  978-1-5310-1255-7


Carolina Academic Press, LLC
700 Kent Street
Durham, North Carolina 27701
Telephone (919) 489-7486
Fax (919) 493-5668
www.cap-press.com
Printed in the United States of America

*Dedicated to Arnold Marmor*

# Contents

# Preface

*Costly Reflections in a Midas Mirror*, Fourth Edition, is a supplementary text to be used near the end of a principles of managerial accounting course or at the beginning of a second-level cost accounting course. This instructional novel is ideal for an MBA program or finance course which has a light coverage of managerial accounting or can be used in CPA firms' or IRS in-house training programs. The book also is suitable for a law school course on managerial accounting or a criminal justice course on white collar crime.

Gerhard G. Mueller, past president of the American Accounting Association, indicates that "malaise" best describes accounting education today. "Our present textbooks and pedagogy haven't changed since the 1950s and are quite obsolete." A scenario approach is one answer to this malaise. A scenario is an example with a character (a person) performing certain actions in a particular situation.

The use of an imaginative novel is an ultimate extension of the scenario approach. A novel can be a series of continuous examples relating to a central theme instead of just several unrelated examples put forth as separate scenarios. In addition, students tend to relate to fictional characters in action-packed adventures. The story, along with its verbal pictures, jogs the memory more easily than gray pages of technical material alone. Proven aids in learning include the element of surprise when a learner encounters an unexpected phenomenon and the retention of a new concept which appears in a dramatic, unusual context.

This novel mixes fraud, murder, art, ethics, humor, cost, and managerial accounting together to provide a better way of learning the managerial accounting process. Lenny Cramer, a professor at Columbia University, tries to help a wealthy friend of his university. As a managerial professor, he uses his forensic accounting background to solve a "whodunit" plot. Along the way, business practices and accounting concepts are elucidated in a way both students and instructors will find gripping as well as informative.

In 1976, L.G. Eckel penned the following:

*There was an accountant*
*who got in a stew.*
*He had so many choices*
*He didn't know what to do.*

The potential murderers are, likewise, numerous in this fast-paced Philip Marlowe-type intrigue. Although a fundamental premise in accounting is that the reporting entity is a going-concern in the absence of evidence to the contrary, with so many murders in this plot, a liquidation assumption is more appropriate. So, jump on board and enjoy the read. Learn how life imitates cost accounting. But keep sunk cost values and salability of assets in mind as you unravel the plot, rather than the traditional historical costs. Remember that an effective managerial accountant must be a good detective and interviewer, even without the fedora and snub-nosed revolver.

We wish to thank Ronald Bagley, Alan Blankley, Marc J. Epstein, Dana Forgione, Jeffrey Kantor, Winston Shearon, Skip Hughes, Joseph Matoney, Arnold Marmor, and Jean Ware.

D. Larry Crumbley
Louisiana State University

Donald L. Ariail
Kennesaw State University

Jeanne M. David
University of Detroit Mercy

Veronica C. Paz
Indiana University of Pennsylvania

*For me, a career in accounting has been like a day in a great orchard with ripe fruit on every tree and insufficient time to taste it all. Opportunities have been overwhelming. Rewards have been more than adequate. I think it will always be so.*

—Robert K. Mautz

*A management accountant applies his or her professional knowledge and skills in the preparation and presentation of financial and other decision-oriented information in such a way as to assist management in the formulation of policies and in the planning and control of the operation of the undertaking.*

—The Institute of Certified Management Accountants (ICMA)

*Most companies, however, use management accounting information derived from the system used to prepare periodic financial statements. Driven by the procedures and cycles of the financial reporting system, most management accounting information is too aggregated, too distorted, and too delayed to be relevant for managerial planning and control. Today's management accounting systems rarely fit contemporary markets and technologies.*

—H. Thomas Johnson and Robert S. Kaplan

*We urge that in order to successfully serve in the dual role of managers/ accountants, management accountants must be prepared to face the challenges of providing management with "classic" and "tailor-made" financial and nonfinancial information. They also must take advantage of the opportunities to expand and enhance their participation in the management process in "traditional" and "world-class" organizations.*

—Grover L. Porter and Michael D. Akers

# Costly Reflections in a Midas Mirror

# One

*The primary focus in a typical budgeting process is on changes to the current operating budget. In contrast, a zero-base-budgeting process allows no activities or functions to be included in the budget unless managers can justify their needs. The amount of work and time needed to perform a true zero-base budgeting on all aspects of operations of an organization can be monumental, however.*

—E.J. Blocher, D.E. Stout, G. Cokins, and K.H. Chen

He was neatly dressed in a business suit even though obviously he was a bodyguard. He was tall and wiry, broad shouldered with brown hair and steely gray eyes. He had a lean tightness about him that showed a no-nonsense attitude. He had a small hairline scar on his forehead. He was the kind you would want on your side in a street fight. If he was carrying a gun, it was cleverly concealed.

I followed him down the gray polished granite corridor to the thick ebony door marked "Chairman." He knocked, keeping his eyes cautiously locked on me, and we both heard a raspy voice bark, "Come in."

He opened the door, held it for me to enter, and then slowly closed it behind me. I heard the heavy latch click, and his footsteps fading as he walked away.

I stood there in Henderson's mammoth office with my back to the closed door, taking in the trappings of power, taking in the gleaming black and ivory oriental furnishings, taking in Henderson.

Lloyd Henderson.

Colossus.

Self-made man, or sharply self-honed image? What's the difference? Probably not quite 70, but sharp and quick in both mind and body.

The look of a savant. Narrow piercing eyes glowered at me, like a cobra. Wisps of white hair clinging to his small, narrow head. A small straight nose over a thin mouth. There was no chin, really. What would a big shot like Henderson want with a chin?

I'd done some quick checking as soon as John S. Burton, the president of my university, told me to help him out. Or rather Hildy, my secretary, did the checking. Three daughters. Two living with him; one thrown out. A twenty-first century King Lear.

His voice was grave. "Professor Cramer. Lenny Cramer?"

I nodded my head. He knew who I was; he'd sent for me. Did he like playing games? He motioned to a leather chair. I walked slowly to the chair and sat down, focusing on my prospective client.

April was dying, and May would be here soon. Mr. Henderson's suit was too heavy for the kind of weather we were having. Black suit, white shirt, and red silk tie. "Recently returned from the Cote d'Azur," he rasped. "Business. And what do I find? Incompetence."

I nodded my head in sympathy.

Henderson squinted at me. "This is a family matter. I want everything handled discreetly. No police involvement. Do you understand?"

"Sure, Mr. Henderson."

"How old are you, Professor Cramer?"

"Forty-three."

"A reliable age. Do you drink?" he snapped.

"Rarely." I wanted to tell him I drank sometimes, but I had the feeling he wouldn't like that answer.

"I never drink," he said. "Impairs your judgment. Do you smoke?"

I was getting tired of off-the-point questions. But what could I do? "Never."

"I don't drink, and I don't smoke. Haven't missed a day of work in fifty-two years," he boasted.

"Why don't you tell me what's on your mind, Mr. Henderson?"

"My granddaughter," he said, "she's gotten off the track. A wild one. Haven't seen her in years, but I've always had a soft spot for her. Her mother, my daughter Myra, came to see me yesterday. She claims Marilyn has taken up with a sordid crowd. She's—uh—living with some artist. In SoHo. I *was* surprised she came here, my daughter, that is. Haven't seen her in years either.

She sat there crying like a baby, wanting my help. Well, I promised her I would—on the condition she would continue to stay away from me."

"There's no embezzlement here?"

He scowled. "Embezzlement? What makes you say that?"

"Just asked. People usually call me when there are financial problems. Wealthy men are targets for embezzlers."

"Nobody cheats me, Professor." He was indignant or was that vindictive. I believed him.

"This daughter who came to see you—her name and address?"

He opened a drawer and gave me a slip of paper.

"And your granddaughter—Marilyn's address?"

"You'll have to get that from Myra," he said. "I told her I would send someone to help and that she should talk to him. She owns a small art gallery."

"Are your other two daughters aware of this—uh—family problem?" I said.

"You know something about me, do you? That I have three daughters?"

"You're an influential man, Mr. Henderson. People with wealth and power are always getting their names in the newspaper. And their backgrounds. This is the Internet and Google age."

"My so-called shady deals," he cackled. He steepled his fingers. "Well, yellow journalism and innuendoes mean nothing. I have two daughters who stay with me and take care of me. The other one, Myra, was incorrigible, and I suppose Marilyn takes after her."

"Uh huh. Now, Mr. Henderson, you wouldn't have contacted John Burton just because your granddaughter is mixed up with a wild crowd. There has to be something more to it."

"Speak to Myra," he said curtly. "She'll tell you what you need to know." He picked up a Mont Blanc pen, and tapped it slowly on his leather desk pad.

"That guy who showed me here to your office. He looks like he could handle this kind of problem." I said almost tongue in cheek.

"Paul? Paul Manfred? Paul is my personal bodyguard. I don't send him out on family errands. Besides, Paul is rather … impulsive."

"If you don't have anything to do with your daughter anymore, what caused the falling out?"

"I don't see how that's of any relevance to you," he snapped, glaring. Then with a tight scowl, "Paul will see you *out*, Mr. Cramer."

I stood up and took my leave. The glass and steel tower I was in was all Henderson's. He was into computers big time. He held several patents for critical silicon and metal-oxide memory chips. He was wealthy all right, a modern-day Midas. Turning sand and rust into gold. But was he developing a flexible, transparent, energy -efficient, lower-cost, hybrid design that was predicted to replace silicon by 2024? That was the billion-dollar question.

What was a Columbia accounting faculty member doing here? I'd made the mistake of telling my university president at a meeting about a year ago that I specialized in art work—hard assets. That was my mistake all right ... and his good memory. Should have kept my mouth shut at that meeting, as that is the first rule of academia.

Burton asked me to help Lloyd Henderson with a delicate family financial problem. Apparently, Henderson donated several million dollars' worth of appreciated artwork to Columbia University under a charitable remainder trust. Great way to reduce taxes, and a great benefit to the university. Too bad I didn't get a piece of that pie in my research and travel budget. Burton figured I might get some consulting work with Henderson's computer company if I helped him out with this problem. The problem was apparently a defective product that did not conform to Henderson's specifications.

All of this adventure was coming on top of the fact I cut my faculty leave short for a miserable toothache. I'd gone to teach principles of business in a private school in Odessa, Ukraine on my sabbatical. I like to travel and visit as many countries as I can. Maybe I like controlled terror—like roller coasters and bungee jumping.

In Kiev, I taught accounting at another State Institute. After that, a group called the Union of Economic Initiatives organized a series of lectures for me throughout the region. Part of the former Soviet Union. Kiev was about 50 miles from the Chernobyl nuclear power plant that blew up in 1986.

I learned that it's common for medical students to bribe their professors in some of the former soviet Republics. Since the average annual salary of an endodontist is 679,563 hryvnia (about $852), dentistry there is what you'd call *primitive*. Two dentists, with six years of experience each, drilled out a filling from the wrong tooth. They wouldn't give me penicillin for my infected gums, because they were afraid it was too dangerous to take penicillin for more than eleven days. They put a temporary filling on the wrong tooth and said good-bye in Russian. That's when I decided to cut my leave short and come back early to the U.S.

Everything was in short supply—housing, cars, food, medicine, surgical gloves, education.... In Odessa there wasn't any water sometimes from midnight to 7:00 A.M.—and hot water was scarce most of the day. Taking a shower was always a gamble. Just when you were all lathered up, you'd get a blast of ice water with no warning. Some cities only had water eight to ten hours a day. What'd you expect, I thought, from a system that had no profit incentive for 70 years? As I told my Soviet audiences, there's only three ways to motivate people—by love, by profit, or by guns. They'd tried guns—it didn't work.

I got my toothache while giving my lecture on break-even analysis. I told the Ukrainian students that the break-even point for a business is the number of units that must be sold to make the total revenues from sales equal the total costs of running the business.

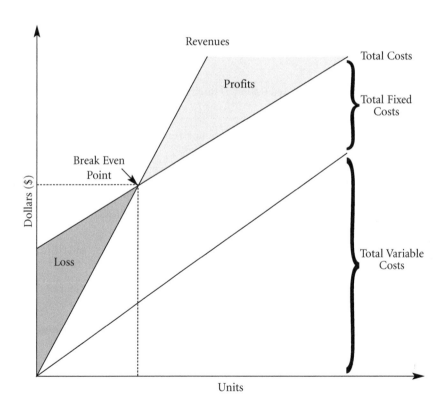

I drew my typical break-even chart on an overhead transparency I'd brought with me. Power point devices were a scarce resource there too. Transparency markers—forget it. They were nowhere to be found there or in the U.S.

I wasn't sure they understood the concept of "relevant range" in my lecture—that variable costs and fixed costs are defined over a certain range of production activity. That is, the behavior of costs, either fixed or variable, holds true over that range of production activity. Relevant range being that of realistic capacity but not optimal.

And I wasn't sure they understood my target profit formulas either.

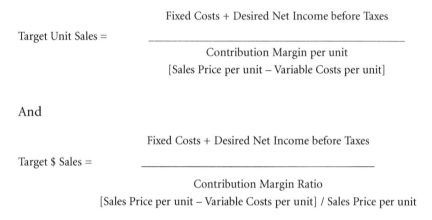

$$\text{Target Unit Sales} = \frac{\text{Fixed Costs} + \text{Desired Net Income before Taxes}}{\substack{\text{Contribution Margin per unit} \\ \text{[Sales Price per unit – Variable Costs per unit]}}}$$

And

$$\text{Target \$ Sales} = \frac{\text{Fixed Costs} + \text{Desired Net Income before Taxes}}{\substack{\text{Contribution Margin Ratio} \\ \text{[Sales Price per unit – Variable Costs per unit] / Sales Price per unit}}}$$

Suppose you manufacture a product that sells for $80. Variable expenses are $50 per unit and total fixed costs for the year will be $45,000. You want to earn $82,000 for the year.

Under the contribution margin method, first calculate the contribution margin.

Contribution margin (CM) is sales price per unit less variable costs per unit or $80 - $50 = $30 per unit.

Then, (Target profit + Fixed expenses) ÷ CM= ($82,000 + $45,000) ÷ $30 = 4233.33

4234 units x $80 = $338,720.

The firm needs to sell 4,234 units if it is going to earn the target profit of $82,000.

Sales will need to be: 4,234 units times $80 = $338,720.

So, to earn an $82,000 profit, 4,234 units must be sold.

I still remember the blank looks on their faces when I told them they should keep producing units, as long as the revenue from sales of the extra units covered their own variable costs, plus at least $1 of fixed costs. I told them that over the long run, all the fixed costs had to be covered by sales of the company's product, if they planned to stay in business. But, in the short-run, any contribution—even $1 a unit toward coverage of the fixed costs, will improve profits, or in their case, reduce losses. Once the break-even point has been achieved, profits are increased if a unit can be sold for more than its variable cost. If the company has not reached its break-even point yet, then any contribution—even $1— will reduce the company's losses. I wonder if they even understood the meaning of "profit?" I did *not* tell them that in the U.S. if you make it, the Feds will take it to cover our huge national debt in the form of taxes.

Well, how was I going to solve Henderson's problem of a defective family? I wasn't even sure what Henderson's problem was. Well, it certainly wasn't going to be solved with break-even analysis—or by whispering sweet debits into somebody's ear.

Outside, I took out the paper Henderson gave me. I punched in Myra Riley's phone number on my cell phone. When she answered I told her I'd be at her place in half an hour.

A cruising cab stopped. I got in and went to Brooklyn. Brooklyn Heights is full of brownstones. The street Mrs. Riley lived on had trees. It looked in good shape for the neighborhood. I paid the driver and bounced up the steps to the building's front door. I buzzed her apartment, and she looked out the window.

"Push in the door, Mr. Cramer, and come on up."

She met me at the top of the stairs. She was somewhere in her early forties, dressed in well-tailored, but noticeably worn, red pants and a pink shirt. She was dark-complexioned, maybe from a tanning bed. We went into her apartment. Much better than the flat where I stayed in Odessa.

The living room was comfortable. Modest furniture, and some oil paintings on the walls.

We sat down in the living room. She told me she was a widow and kept her husband's name. "I do not know what to do about my daughter Marilyn."

"What exactly is the problem?" I asked. I was getting a little impatient with the lack of information.

"This is so ... embarrassing."

"It usually is."

"Would you like a drink?"

"No thanks. What problem is Marilyn having?" So far, my time would have been better spent working in my office on that never-ending research project.

If she had a handkerchief in her hands it would look as if she would've torn it to shreds. Even a junior auditor could see how nervous she was.

"Marilyn is 20. She likes to think she's an adult. Of course, she *is*. But sometimes she acts like a child—just oblivious to how she affects other people. She's always been rebellious—"

"She's 20, and she's a big girl," I said. "You went to your father for help. What kind of help do you need?"

"I own a small art gallery. Marilyn helps me in the gallery. She does all the bookkeeping. I think she may be taking money." She paused for a moment. "But I can't be sure."

One person controlling the books—typical small business. Inwardly, I shook my head. The first principle of internal control is always having *segregation of duties*. Never let the same person safeguard the cash and keep the books—there's too much temptation and opportunity for embezzlement.

No one should have the opportunity to perpetuate a fraud and cover it up. For example, anyone receiving cash or having the custody of assets should not oversee accounting for it. That is why the Treasurer in a company should receive cash receipts, while the accounting department headed by the Controller should account for the cash (e.g., bank reconciliations), but never have access to it.

It even happens among family members. When two or more people divide the financial tasks, any misappropriation of funds requires collusion. Of course, workers might collude. But the more people involved, the less likely a "successful" collusion will happen. Of course, more than 40 people knew about the $12 billion fraud at WorldCom. A number of people knew about Bernard Madoff's $64 **billion** Ponzi scheme.

I knew an organization that allowed the same controller to handle all its finances for more than forty years—the typical trusted employee. During the last years of his career he developed some medical problems that were expensive to treat. He had a need—the so-called motive and *pressure*—and he had the *opportunity* to steal. All he needed was a *rationalization*. Usually they kid themselves into thinking they'll pay it all back once they get on their feet again. These three components are the fraud triangle.

When a new president took over the organization, some uncomfortable financial questions were asked, and over the course of the next two months a total of $240,000 appeared out of nowhere back in the company's cash accounts. No sales, no transfers from other accounts, and no loan proceeds could account for the inflow. Guess the treasurer decided to put some of the embezzled money back. Or, maybe he just went out and borrowed enough to cover the obvious shortages—and quiet the questions—while he waited for an opportunity to steal the money back again to pay off his loans.

Not likely Marilyn would run a sophisticated embezzlement scheme. But then again, what did I know about Marilyn Riley?

Myra's eyes were fixed on mine. She had great eyes. "She's involved with this ... boy. He's an artist. He's on drugs—I *know* it. She poses for him. And ... and ..."

She looked away. "Marilyn is involved in some kind of a theft. She might go to jail. I'm so afraid—"

"How do you know that?" I leaned forward.

"She *bragged* about it," Myra said. "She was here, two days ago, and bragged about stealing something big. I think she'd been drinking. If she gets caught—she'll go to jail. She's my daughter. I know she's out of control, but I have to do something to help her."

"What did she steal? Art work from your shop? Cash from the register?"

"I don't think she did the stealing herself. It was that boyfriend of hers, Teddy Noren. He works part-time in the gallery too."

"Did you tell all of this to your father?"

"Well, yes. He has always liked Marilyn. I was sure he would help her. I have no real money, Mr. Cramer. I knew I'd need his help. A lawyer or a private detective or something."

"I'm not a detective, just a forensic accounting professor. Now do you have any idea what was stolen? I might be able to help you."

"I don't know. She didn't say. She just kept going on about how she was going to get a million dollars."

"You didn't question her about it?"

"Well, of course. But it was no use. She just giggled like when she was a little girl, and then took off. She was almost hysterical."

"You think this Teddy Noren is involved?"

"Oh, I'm sure of it. They're very close. I'm so worried."

"You'd better take something for your nerves," I said. "You'll go to pieces, and that won't help your daughter any." I leaned back and stretched. "You got an address and phone number for Teddy Noren? Maybe a cell phone number? I'll talk to him."

"It's in my address book. In the kitchen." She left the room and came back with a pad and pencil and the address book. She found the address and number and wrote it down for me.

"Your daughter there now?"

"I don't know. She might be. Or she might be working somewhere for one of the local artists. She poses for them on the side."

"What was the falling-out between you and your father?" I asked.

"I don't see —"

"Just curious."

"Twenty years ago, I met George Riley. I fell in love with him, but my father said he was a fortune hunter. I think my father only wanted me to stay at home and take care of him. He's like that. He uses overdependence and his illnesses to control ... all of us. He's an expert at manipulating the guilt feelings of his daughters. I just couldn't live with it any more. Do you know what it's like to live with unrelenting criticism all your life? I insisted on marrying George, so he wrote me out of his will, and just about disowned me. After my husband died I tried to see my father again, but he refused. I visited him a few times for holidays in later years, but he has always made me feel unwelcome. I've never asked him for anything. Just — just to see him, to remind him he had another daughter beside those two witches who stay with him. The only reason he even talked to me the other day was because Marilyn was in trouble."

"He says he's healthy as a horse. You don't get along with your two sisters?"

"We hate each other. I think Cora and Sandra hate each other. Oh, what does it matter. He's a vindictive man, Professor Cramer. I think the three of them thrive on their mutually exploitive existence in that ... house."

"Yes." I stood up. "What does it matter?"

# Two

*Managers need not — and should not — abandon the effort to justify computer integrated manufacturing on financial grounds. Instead, they need ways to apply the discounted cash flow approach more appropriately.*

—Robert S. Kaplan

I ate lunch in a corner deli on Metropolitan Avenue, and then I took a taxi back to Manhattan. The air was warm. People were starting to wear lighter clothes. When we got to SoHo, the driver kept an eye peeled for Prince Street.

"Easier to get around here than in the Village," he said. "Here it is."

The four story, dingy, brown, brick apartment building was crammed between an art store and a shop that sold silver jewelry. A whiff of back alley stench greeted me as I walked in the front door. One of the cluster mail boxes had a faded card taped near it that read "Noren/Riley." The card had 302 written on it. I went up three flights of filthy wooden stairs. A drug dealer's heaven, I thought. The door to number 302 was open about an inch. There was the faint smell of cordite coming from the apartment.

"Trouble?" I said half out loud and pushed the door open with my elbow. When I was inside the small apartment I pushed the door back with my other elbow.

Half the living room was set up like an art studio. There was a wooden easel, with a painting resting on it. A nearby table was cluttered with tubes of paint, brushes, small pallet knives for textured painting, and rags. I noticed a couple of small bottles of linseed oil next to the paints. A chair was on its side. On the floor between the chair and the easel lay the folded body of a young

13

man. He was on his left side, his face turned up. Dispassionate, stark eyes—a face that was blanched and rigid, framed with short-cropped brown hair. He was dressed in baggy black pants. His chest and feet were cold, white, and bare. He looked like someone who'd fallen asleep with their eyes open. There was a small trickle of blood still coming from his right temple, pooling on the dirty brown carpet on the floor. Near his hand was a .38 revolver. I carefully checked for a pulse. None. Could they get my fingerprints?

No sign of a struggle. It looked like he was sitting on the chair, and then for reasons only he knew, put the gun to his head and squeezed the trigger. So, he was on the floor from the force of the bullet, and the chair went with him. One more wasted life. Looked like an unmistakable case of suicide. But I'm not CSI.

Now what was the problem?

I looked at the painting. Suicide. That just didn't make sense. I touched the back tip of a knuckle to a corner of the painting, and it was slightly wet. The brush strokes were short and uncertain. I thought I recognized the subject. A fresh forgery? Maybe. But, then again, sometimes artists train by copying famous masterpieces.

I looked at the tubes of paint, rolled them around with the back of my fingers on the table thinking.

I went through the rest of the apartment. No more tubes of paint. I was getting edgy by now. Suicide would suit me fine—no mess, no entanglements. I went through the apartment one more time. Living room, bedroom, kitchen, and bathroom. I even looked under the bed. If anyone had seen me I would have looked quite foolish. But I was starting to feel some unexplained sense of desperation about this whole affair. It was like I *wanted* this situation to turn out to be a suicide.

The only items in the bedroom that seemed like they didn't belong were two digital laboratory scales. An open box of grocery store paraffin—old-fashioned white laundry wax—sat on top of the dresser. A couple of chunks of wax the size on my thumb were sitting on one of the scales.

Where was Marilyn? Posing? Shopping? I couldn't stay in this apartment for long, not with a dead artist for company.

I used my handkerchief to wipe off everything I might have touched and went downstairs. A thought bothered me. Could the police get my fingerprints off the body where I felt for the pulse? Had I left my DNA? Maybe a hair?

I walked into the nearby art store. There was a painting that took up an entire wall. An abstract. Looked like someone threw buckets of different colored paint on the canvas. Must have taken a lot of skill to do that. Smaller paintings hung on the other walls. Acrylics, oils, and a few watercolors.

A young woman, probably in her 20s, wearing a black blazer over black leggings, and a pair of Doc Martens gave me a smile. Deep circles under her eyes. She pointed to a table that carried a bottle of white wine, and some paper cups. I shook my head. "No thanks."

"I'm looking for somebody," I said. "Marilyn Riley. Maybe you know her. She lives next door."

"If she lives next door," she said, "why don't you go up and see her?"

"Nobody home."

"Well, how can I help you?"

"If you know her …"

"I know Marilyn."

"You have any idea where she might be now?"

"She's probably at her mother's art gallery, or with a photographer. Isn't Teddy home? Teddy Noren?"

"I knocked, but there was no answer," I lied.

The girl was getting obviously bored. "What do you want me to do about it?"

"I wonder if you'd mind answering a few questions. I'm not police. Just someone who's looking for her."

"I think I do mind, Mr.…."

"Stanley. J.D. Stanley." Lying always made me feel uneasy.

"Mr. Stanley, I'm afraid I can't help you. I know Marilyn, and I know Teddy. I like them. And I don't like nosy people. Now if you'll excuse me …"

"I don't mean to be nosy."

"All right," she said. "So, you're not nosy. Now will you please leave?"

Sometimes you get a hit; sometimes you strike out. I struck out.

I made a slight nod. "Whatever you like. One question that can't hurt anybody. Is there an art supply store near here?"

"Go up to West Broadway, and turn right, one block."

"Thanks." I made my retreat.

If the police questioned her, she'd remember me. Bad news for me. Even if the police decided it was suicide, they'd probably question her, just as a neighbor. Routine. And they'd look for Marilyn Riley, the dead man's lover. I wanted to see Marilyn before the police got to her.

I had better results at the next art supply store. Sketch pads, china pencils, brushes, easels, and paints. All high volume items. There's two basic strategies in retail operations—high margin, low turnover, or low margin, high turnover.

An item's **margin** is the amount of its sales price left after the cost of the item is subtracted. *Turnover* is the speed with which an item of inventory moves through a business. The amount of time it takes from receipt of the item from a supplier until the item is sold to a customer is turnover. For instance, low margin inventory in a grocery store turns over quickly, while the high margin inventory in a jewelry store turns over slowly.

The **inventory turnover ratio** is cost of goods sold divided by the average inventory. Discount stores depend on high turnover of merchandise inventory, while hospitals suffer from slow turnover of accounts receivable, not collecting the money from the customer.

The same turnover concept applies to all the balance sheet items. They're all "inventories"—that is, inventory of cash, inventory of merchandise, inventory of receivables, inventory of equipment. Both the fast and slow turnover strategies can be equally efficient from a Return on Investment (ROI) standpoint, but you must match the strategy with the nature of the product market.

In an art supply store like this one, a high margin, slow turnover strategy would leave the owner with a few sales, and a lot of dried-out paint sitting on the shelves. That approach would be better for a gallery, where they sell a few, high-priced paintings.

Of course, gross margin is the difference between sales revenue and cost of goods sold. This concept shows how much a business is making on the mark-up of the units sold—that is, before the deduction of operating expenses.

This concept of mark-up can be confusing. Suppose Walmart buys sheets for \$25 and marks them up by 75%. The sales price becomes \$43.75 (\$25 times 1.75). The cost of goods sold is \$25, and the \$18.75 (\$43.75 minus \$25) over and above the cost to Walmart is unit margin—not profit.

The shop was crowded. There were artists and students looking at items and buying supplies. I finally cornered a middle-aged looking gentleman wearing a tweed jacket, with patches on the elbows. Balding. Slender, with oval glasses.

"Teddy Noren recommended me," I told the sales clerk.

"Oh, yes. Mr. Noren. Nice chap. Good artist. I've seen his work."

"He said he gets his oils from you."

The sales clerk looked puzzled. "Oils? Oh no, no, he never buys oils from me. Acrylics. That's what Teddy uses mostly, at least as far as I know."

I thanked the man and left.

Back to Myra Riley. She had an anxious look in her eyes. Her nerves looked considerably worse than when I'd seen her before. We sat down, facing each other. "Marilyn is not home?" I asked.

"You could have called me," she said.

"You didn't see Teddy Noren today, did you?"

Her face dropped to a sharp frown. "What? Of course not. What kind of question is that?"

I looked at her, and said, "Mind if I have a glass of water?" She got up without answering, and I watched her go to the kitchen.

She handed me the glass and sat down again. She hadn't made a drink for herself. "Why did you ask if I'd seen Teddy?"

"Just asking. I was in his apartment. You're sure he's on drugs?"

"Yes. I'm sure."

"I didn't see Marilyn, either."

"Did you talk to Teddy?" she said anxiously.

"Tried to. I'd planned to. But he wasn't talking. You know how it is when you're dead."

She gasped. Her face went ashen white, her eyes bulging.

"It looked like suicide," I said.

"What! Suicide?" She was attempting to regain control. Gulped. "Suicide? But he was so young. Why? What reason would he have to kill himself?"

"I don't know, Myra. I didn't know him. You'd know about his problems better than I would."

"What about Marilyn?" she asked anxiously.

"Uh, what about *me*? I was in that apartment. Somebody might have seen me go into that building. What if the police find me, and start asking me questions? What am I going to tell *them*? About Marilyn and this million-dollar rip-off they were up to?"

"Tell them nothing," she said crisply, lifting her face. Her nostrils flared. "They can't make you tell them anything, can they?"

"What are you, a lawyer?" I asked.

"Of course not."

"Then I guess they can do whatever they want," I replied.

She wrung her hands, and I wondered if she'd known Teddy Noren was dead before she gave me his address.

"Did they really steal something?" I said, wanting to get back to the reason I got involved in this engagement in the first place.

Her anger flashed this time. "I told you, didn't I? What are you trying to imply?"

"But you don't know what they stole?"

"No. I don't see—"

I stood up. "Never mind, Mrs. Riley. I want to see Marilyn—before the police do."

She also stood up and stepped close to me. Closer than she needed to. She lifted the glass out of my hand. "I'm sorry, Lenny," she said looking up into my eyes. "Thank you for trying to help Marilyn. Please, call me Myra." Those beautiful eyes again.

"All right, Myra." This lady was riding an emotional whipsaw.

"If Marilyn should call you, have her call my office. Here's my business card."

"Please don't think I'm holding out on you," she purred. "I am being honest with you."

"Of course." Was this Pollyannaism, or Judy Garland playing Dorothy in the Wizard of Oz?

"There's doubt in your voice," she observed.

"It's because of the business I'm in. Every accountant must exercise *professional skepticism*. Trust, but verify. I'll check back with you later tonight."

She saw me to the door. I couldn't place that perfume. Passion, I think. I didn't remember it from my visit earlier in the day.

I went down to look for a taxi to my office on campus—four cabs passed by before one finally stopped. I climbed in. I could still smell Myra's perfume as we drove.

Luca Turin, a perfume critic and author says that "perfume is a message in a bottle. It's not a smell. It's an impression, an idea." I wonder if cost accounting is somewhat like perfume. I believe I'll use this concept as an essay question on my next graduate exam.

# Three

*Standard costing systems enhance planning and control and improve performance measurement. Standard costing systems also provide readily available unit cost information that can be used for pricing decisions at any time throughout the period because actual costs (either direct or indirect) do not need to be known.*

— D.L. Heitger, M.M. Mowen, and D.R. Hansen

18. What type of total cost will change in direct proportion to changes in activity level?
    a. sunk cost
    b. fixed cost
    c. variable cost
    d. opportunity cost
    e. some other answer

I circled "c. variable cost," the right answer. I was reviewing the undergraduate cost accounting exam I would give to my students at the end of the week. As usual, on multi-choice exams the answer was "c." Of course, total fixed costs do not change with a change in the quantity of the cost driver, within the relevant range and a given period of time (e.g., one year).

I needed to be more careful. On a multiple-choice exam with five possible answers, a student with no knowledge should by chance be able to correctly answer one in five of the questions and thereby score 20 points. With the knowledge that c was the most frequent answer, even a fine arts major could score better than 20 on a cost accounting exam just by the law of averages. Or for that matter, even a monkey should score about a 50 on a true-false exam.

I put my pocket calendar, iPad, and a map into my leather brief case. The case I bought in Hong Kong. I kept it because it reminded me of Dana Scott, and my Burmese visit. Of course, it is called Myanmar now. Painful memories of my first real relationship, after the death of my wife, came rushing back to me. Dana was still in jail for attempting to steal ancient treasures out of the Burma Stupa in Rangoon. That seemed like a long time ago now. I wished I could get back to Thailand. Those times with Dana still hit emotions I hadn't felt in years.

I finished proofing the cost accounting exam and hid it in the bottom left drawer of my desk. After finding my teaching notes, I left my sixth-floor office and took the elevator to Watson library on the first floor. Uris Hall has eight floors. Our business library is well maintained, and well-staffed. Something that has paid off for me more than once on my research, and on my consulting engagements.

I'd left my old copy of the October 1991 issue of *Management Accounting* at home, so I photocopied one at the library. The journal is now called *Strategic Finance*, a publication of the Institute of Management Accounting. In that issue, Robert Koehler asserted that a combination of activity-based costing, direct costing, and the contribution margin approach, would give a true overview of a company's whole cost picture. Well, that was an improvement, I guess.

Cost reports get distorted by including indirect, noncontrollable costs, using blunt and arbitrary allocation methods. There's few things more discouraging than holding managers responsible for costs over which they have no control. Our university president would be wasting his time if he tried to hold faculty members like me responsible for cost control on the construction of a parking garage at the university. Sorry. But faculty members have no control or authority over parking garage construction expenditures. While activity-based costing is a major refinement of indirect cost allocation methods such as those used in absorption costing, it still boils down to arbitrary decisions about what business activities *drive* what costs, and how to measure and apply those cost relationships in the real world.

Product pricing decisions based on unit costs that include over or under allocations of indirect cost, can have devastating effects on the price competitiveness of the entire company. If production of a certain titanium jet engine part requires three machine-tool setups, but only one direct labor hour, then using a traditional cost driver like *direct labor hours* to apply overhead costs will understate the real cost of making that part. Prices based on cost will be too low, and as a result the company will lose money on sales of the jet engine part. The number of machine-tool setups should be used as the cost driver for allocating costs to that jet engine part — especially if the cost of a machine-tool setup is much higher than the cost of a direct labor hour.

Worse yet, the company can end up with too many orders and sales for that titanium jet engine just because they have underpriced it using direct labor hours as the overhead application rate. But the firm's total overhead is still being incurred, and the low overhead assigned to the titanium jet engine results in applying too much cost to other products they produce. These other products will not look profitable, and the company will increase those prices and eventually lose sales to other companies. This peanut butter pricing, as it is often called, can cause a firm to focus its efforts on producing and selling products which in reality are the lower margin products.

I headed for my afternoon class. I began my lecture once again by clearing my throat. The students slowly quieted down, and their conversations came to a halt. I casually scanned the aggregation of students in the cost accounting class.

With my usual deadpan tone, I began with, "You all, of course, have read the chapter and done the homework assignments for today."

Some students nodded their heads. Some looked disinterested in the way this class — every class — began. Some students were reading the independent *Columbia Daily Spectator*, the student newspaper.

As the room became quiet, I asked more enthusiastically, "What then, is a *variable* cost? Pretend I'm your friend majoring in art history. How would you explain variable cost to me?"

A heavy-set young man in the front row raised his hand. I nodded in his direction. "Yes, Jake," I said.

"Variable costs are costs that change in relation to increases or decreases in an activity, like units of production."

I smiled. "Exactly. What are some examples?"

The same student responded, "Direct material costs usually increase as units of production increase. So, they would be a variable cost. On the other hand, a supervisor's salary is constant, it wouldn't change with fluctuations in units of production."

"Good. So what kind of cost is the supervisor's salary?"

"Fixed cost," the student responded.

"Does everyone agree with that answer?" I asked the class at large.

A few students nodded. The majority of the class responded with blank looks on their faces.

"Okay, let's take a vote. How many agree that a cost that doesn't change with fluctuations in an activity level is a *fixed* cost? Raise your hand."

Most students raised a hand.

I continued. "So, most of you agree that the supervisor's salary is a *fixed* cost. Therefore, the supervisor's salary doesn't change with the production level."

A few of the students nodded their heads. But one student in the back of the room raised her hand.

"Yes?" I asked, looking toward her, sitting in the right rear corner of the large classroom. "Go ahead."

"Well, a fixed cost is fixed only in relation to a given period of time and a specific range of activity."

"Excellent. That's exactly right. While the supervisor's salary is considered a fixed cost, when the production level increases beyond a certain range, then the firm will have to hire a second supervisor. Hiring a second supervisor would double the cost of the supervisors' salaries. For example, a manufacturing company running one assembly line eight hours a day, might only need one supervisor. If the company expands to two eight-hour shifts, they'll need to hire a second supervisor to supervise the second shift. That's what we call a 'step' fixed cost. It increases in discrete 'chunks' like the steps of a staircase."

He paused and looked around. No hands. "O.K., the riser on the staircase is the 'chunk,' or the increase in the cost, or the added cost of one more supervisor. The level of activity during which the cost is not changing is the tread or landing for each step. So, a single tread (first step) is represented by the need for only one supervisor. At the point where the production activity requires a second shift and second supervisor, we arrive at the second step. Of course, not all step costs take on the form of a nice neat staircase. Some will have uneven risers, that are uneven increases in costs. Others will have short or long treads; that is, the production activity level where the cost changes may be uneven. If the treads are relatively long like the production level that can be achieved without the addition of a second shift, the cost can be considered fixed within the relative range of one shift."

He stopped again to get his breath. "On the other hand, if the 'chunks' are relatively small like the addition of an eight hour per day maintenance worker, the cost can be considered variable. The 'relative range' is the span of activity within which our assumptions about cost behavior remain valid. By plotting a graph of the expected cost over the relevant range, the firm can see how the cost looks. Lots of steps within the relevant range can be approximated as a variable or mixed cost. No steps in the relevant range can be estimated as a fixed cost. A few significant steps in the relevant range may best have several cost estimates with the cost being treated as fixed, but only for a portion of the relevant range. A company may feel that its relevant range is 10,000 to 15,000 units, and a particular cost is fixed only if production falls between 12,000 and 14,000 units. Essentially, management needs to know if production is going to be under 12,000 units or over 14,000 units, the cost must be re-evaluated."

"Can anyone think of another reason a fixed cost like the supervisor's salary might change?" he asked.

A student sitting in the middle of the room spoke out. "If it's a good union, they'll negotiate higher pay at the next collective bargaining session." Several students laughed.

I smiled. "That's a good point. Changes can occur in *fixed* costs over time. Like you said, the union might bargain for a higher compensation package in their next contract. The rent on a building is usually considered a fixed cost relative to production, but from year to year, the cost may be negotiable, depending on the terms of the lease."

"What do we mean by *total* fixed cost and *average* fixed cost per unit?" I asked.

The student on the front row, who'd responded to the first question, raised his hand again.

I nodded in his direction. The student began, "The total amount paid to the supervisor in a given period is the total cost of the supervisor's salary. If you divide that by the number of units produced, you get the average cost per unit. Since a supervisor's salary is fixed, the total cost doesn't change, regardless of whether the production volume goes up or down. On the other hand, the average cost of the supervisor's salary per unit will go up or down as the production level goes up or down."

"Excellent. There's an inverse relationship between the average fixed cost per unit of activity and the level of activity, such as units of production. That's what economies of scale are all about. The higher the production volume, the lower the average fixed cost per unit. We spread the fixed costs out thinner over a greater number of units. That's why hospitals and universities are so sensitive to patient volume or student enrollments. They're both high fixed cost operations. Volume means everything in terms of being able to reduce average per unit costs. What about total and average *variable* costs?"

A second-row student raised her hand this time.

I motioned toward the student with my right hand. She responded. "Average variable cost per unit stays the same no matter what the production level. The total variable cost increases or decreases as the production level increases or decreases."

"Great!" I replied. "*Average* variable cost per unit is constant as the activity level changes, but *total* variable cost changes in direct proportion to changes in the activity level."

I was happy. I loved teaching, and especially teaching students who responded actively to questions in class. But students seem to study less and less every year. Their average age is going up. And so are their family and career responsibilities. They've got less time than ever to keep up with their course work. There's also been grade inflation over the years, no doubt because of the widespread use of student evaluation of teacher surveys (SETs).

I am amazed at the reduction in course coverage by other faculty as they try every angle to improve their course evaluation scores. I call it SET management. Corporate executives go to prison if they manage earnings, but professors are rewarded and promoted if they engage in SET management.

One faculty member told me to "entertain them, reduce coverage, make it easy, and make them think they've learned something. That's the key. Make them think they've learned something. Obviously, easy exams are essential." Maybe he never learned the rule—quality doesn't cost, it pays.

I tried to teach my students how to use the course material in real life. Cost or managerial accounting gave students the tools they needed to analyze and solve complex, unstructured business problems. I emphasized different types of problem solving, rather than memorizing routine calculations.

I know the left side of the brain will dominate most of the students who self-select into our accounting programs. So, I try to get them to use the right side of their brain, by using vivid metaphors, parables, pictures, loud noises, colors, and music. I used examples of real business cases from my forensic accounting and consulting practice and required my students to read a cost accounting action adventure novel. I told my students that "half the brain of every student is neglected. The *left* side of the brain understands technology, and the *right* side of the brain sees how it fits into the total picture."

To encourage thinking with both sides of their brains, I usually flash a PowerPoint slide on the screen during my first class that says:

| LEFT SIDE | RIGHT SIDE |
|---|---|
| • logical side | • creative side |
| • verbalizes | • nonverbal |
| • analyzes | • intuition |
| • abstracts | • leaps of insight |
| • marks time | • dreaming |
| • counts | • understands metaphors |
| • plans | • subjective |
| • makes rational statements | • relational |
| • logic | • holistic |
| | • time-free mode |
| | • creates new combinations of ideas |

During most of my exams I left a slide on the screen that said:
- I am not a bean counter.
- I have imagination.
- I will use the right side of my brain!
- I am creative.
- I will be a forensic accountant.

Three or four times during a class I may ask the students to hold their finger on their right nostril and breathe through their left one. Breathing through their left nostril is supposed to stimulate the right side of their brain—or so I'm told.

I tell them they need to think creatively to solve ambiguous problems. We all have a high need for closure. That's why we study accounting. We like everything to balance. We like to foot and cross-foot, so everything checks, and we get the right answer. We believe in Pacioli's instruction "that a person should not go to sleep at night until the debits equal the credits." If we didn't have a high need for closure, we'd all be artists.

My claim to fame was forensic accounting or litigation support services. The American Institute of Certified Public Accountants defines a forensic accountant as a fraud auditor, or an investigative accountant who searches for evidence of criminal conduct or assists in the determination of, or rebuttal of, claimed damages in a legal dispute. They help lawyers. Much of my outside income was from plaintiffs or defendants and their lawyers. They hire me to provide investigative accounting services, prepare financial analyses in support of their cases, provide depositions, and serve as an expert witness in court. I was a formidable opponent for the other attorney to cross-examine. It paid well. But you need a thick hide. It's not a sideline for the faint-hearted.

Now I did more than just disputed divorce settlement work. My areas included litigation support for anti-trust analysis, professional malpractice, locating hidden assets, loss determination, reimbursement, corporate compliance, general consulting, and cost allocation. Anytime someone had to dig into the corpse of records, I was available. Super accountant Cramer! Maybe I should get a special cape to wear like Superman. Or was that Batman? I pack a notebook PC.

* * *

I thought about my daughter Rebecca, while taking the subway across town to my second office. When I left Atlanta to accept my professorship at Columbia University, Rebecca was 17, and became a first-year student at Duke University in Durham, N.C. She is a computer systems and business major. Not an accountant yet like her old man. She called me the other night from one of the computer centers, where she was doing her homework. She was probably checking out the boys, too. I smiled, as I stepped off the subway platform, and thought of my old days as one of those cyberian pinheads— what we used to call the students who just ate bags of peanuts out of the candy machine and ran boxes of dot-matrix printouts all night on the Cyber 150 mainframes. Fun times.

I checked my Fitbit. Only 7,322 steps. Still a long way to go to get my 10,000 steps today.

Good thing I walk around in the classroom.

# Four

*Today, the scene is changing. Once again, managers are beginning to manage their companies rather than just the numbers. Many are doing it to survive, others because they recognize they must adapt to the new manufacturing environment if they are to maintain their competitive edge.*

—C.J. McNair and William Mosconi

John Grant, with his skeletal face, sat behind his desk. Hands folded in front of him. He listened to what I had to say. He was close to 60, lean as a reed, but wiry and active. John was the principal owner of a small forensic accounting practice that specialized in business fraud-related investigations. I was his silent partner. So, I had done consulting for his firm on a number of occasions.

"Look John, I don't have time for this project. I need you to help bail me out of it." I told him the few details I knew.

"You think this Myra Riley just gave you a line and nothing else?" he quizzed. "What would be her motive? You know, motive, opportunity, and rationalization. The old fraud triangle."

"I don't know."

"She might be telling you the truth."

"I'll know more when I talk to her daughter."

"Well, Mrs. Riley's father is paying the bills," Grant said. "And he is Lloyd Henderson. *The* Lloyd Henderson. He has the dough—and a he's a heavy donor to your school. We're not going to question his daughter's veracity if he keeps paying the bills. What makes you think her boyfriend might have been murdered?"

"The painting in his apartment," I said. "The canvas was still wet. I touched it. Oil. A copy of Bellini's *Madonna*. But all the tubes of paint on his table were acrylics. The brush strokes didn't look like experienced work. I went through the apartment. No tubes of oils. Acrylic would have dried faster. I checked an art supply store where he gets his paint. He always buys acrylics. Somebody worked on that canvas. Maybe that somebody brought their own case of oils, worked on the canvas, and then left. Before or after murdering Teddy Noren. There were bottles of linseed oil there. Linseed is used to thin oil paints, not acrylics."

"Still no reason to believe it's a murder," Grant grumbled.

"Nope, doesn't have to be. So, call it a feeling. Intuition. My gut! Fraud is sometimes found by intuition alone."

"And suppose it was a murder, why would the killer work on a painting set up in Noren's apartment?"

"I don't know. Maybe to establish an alibi or something. At this point, I don't know."

"Well, this person would have to be really stupid. The police experts would see the painting was a copy. So, how much do we tell Henderson?"

"As far as I can tell, Myra Riley is my client," I said. "But if I do have to see Henderson, I will. Like you said, he's the one that's paying the bills."

I went to my cramped office. Passed our secretary, who was busy on the phone, and gave her a small wink. I kept a desk at the accounting firm. I was a 15 percent silent partner. My department head at Columbia did know much about my double life. Professor by day, forensic accountant by night. Maybe someday they'll make a TV action series about me, *CSI Accountants*. After all, there was a series called, *LA Law* and the many CSI series. Accountants certainly lead a more exciting life than lawyers. How about *The Auditors*, kind of like *The Doctors*? No. Doctors make more than I do. It would probably end up being more like a soap opera, *General Ledger*.

Our office was a little different from many accounting firms. With our roster of personal and business fraud cases, our accounting investigators made use of notebook computers, forensic software, Internet searches, and online data bases. Our investigators comb dozens of online data sources, like credit reports, probate records, court dockets, marriage and divorce records, motor vehicle records, and several Internet phone directories and lists with identifying information. Works great for skip tracing. We can load government mag tapes right off their mainframes, onto our PC workstations when we need them.

She breezed into my office a few minutes later. Hildy was less than 40. Slim, with shoulder length, chestnut hair. Her skirt was lime, and her blouse was lemon. She had been my secretary for several years. She sat down across from me, "So you met the mighty Lloyd Henderson? What did you think?" she asked.

"Ice water in his veins. More like freon. Ruthless. He lives for money."

"It seems to me he could have retired a long time ago, but he probably couldn't stand giving up control of his company. He works to dominate the memory chip market, so he can make more millions. I wouldn't want to cross him in a business deal," Hildy said.

"How do you know so much about him? And where did you get it?"

Hildy sniffed, with a sly smile. "You spend too much time in the ivory tower Lenny. From what I've read, he controls his public image carefully. I suspect that when he's not hauling other companies over a barrel to design circuit cards that work best with his memory chips, he stays at home, with two of his devoted daughters. I hear that if other companies don't optimize their cards for interface with his chips, he tweaks his design, so their cards won't work right when they're plugged into a motherboard."

"Nice guy. Threw his third daughter out of the house," I said. "King Lear, and his three daughters."

"That's about it, Professor. Somebody wanted to do an unauthorized biography of him one time. Word got to Henderson. After all, the author had to do a lot of digging and ask a lot of questions. Well he ended up in a hospital. Two broken legs. Somebody 'explained' Henderson's position on biographies to him in a back alley. There went the great exposé."

"And nothing proven against Henderson?"

"Fight the rich and powerful?" Hildy lifted her well-shaped eyebrows, green eyes twinkling, "The idealists are dying out. Investigative reporters are disappearing."

"Do me a favor, will you Hildy? Order me a turkey club sandwich and a Coke from the deli across the street. Better have them send it up."

"Why not?" She got up. "Large or small?"

"Small, thanks."

I thought and waited for the food ... and a phone call. When the food arrived, I ate my sandwich and drank my dose of caramel colored phosphoric acid and caffeine. Sugar loaded, of course. The phone rang.

A feminine voice, frightened. "Mr. Cramer?"

I asked if it was Marilyn.

"Yes, my mother …"

"Don't say anything. Are you in your apartment on Prince Street?"

"Yes."

"Get over here right away." I gave her my office address and hung up.

She arrived in less than half an hour.

Marilyn Riley, granddaughter of the great Lloyd Henderson. A blue-eyed blonde of 20, tall and skinny, wearing loose blue jeans and a man's black dress shirt, sat down. Her sunken eyes and the ashen fright on her face were telling.

"He's dead, Mr. Cramer. Teddy's *dead*."

"You found him and called your mother. That's right?"

"Yes."

"Have you called the police yet?"

"No. I'll have to, won't I?"

"Yes. But not yet."

Puzzled she asked, "Wh … what do you mean?"

"I want to talk to you first."

"About what? Teddy's dead. I, I saw the gun—"

"Ever seen that gun before?"

"Yes. It's Teddy's."

"Did he ever talk to you about killing himself?"

"Killing himself? No … But I guess—"

"What time did you leave the apartment?"

"This morning? About nine."

"Was anyone else in the apartment beside Teddy?"

"No," was the quick response.

"Was he expecting anyone?"

"Well, he said he might meet Bram before lunch. I guess he didn't."

"Who's Bram?"

"Bram Walker. A friend of ours. He paints—or he tries to. Landscapes. And other things."

"Oils or acrylic?"

"Oils," she sighed absently. "I don't see—"

"When you went to visit your mother, you told her you were involved in some kind of a theft."

She bit her lower lip. "My mother's a pain. She's not big on my life style. So, I thought I'd —"

I interrupted her again. "Then there was no theft?"

"No, of course not. I was only giving her a hard time."

"Great," I scowled. "Go on back to your apartment, call the police. And tell them you got home and found Teddy Noren dead. I'd appreciate it if you didn't mention me to the police, Miss Riley."

"What do I do then?"

"Go on with your life. Since there was no theft, and you aren't in any trouble, you don't need my services."

She looked bewildered by my remark.

"Your mother thought you were in some kind of financial trouble," I explained. "She went to your grandfather. He contacted the president of my university, looking for someone who could handle a family business financial problem as quietly as possible, and I went to see your grandfather. He gave me your mother's number. I went to visit her, and she told me you were involved in a possible theft. Some mothers worry too much. Since there's no embezzlement, no theft of assets, and you haven't done anything to get into trouble, then you don't need my services. It's that simple."

"Then why did you ask me all those questions?"

"Just trying to make sure it was a suicide. From what everything looks like, it probably is. I'm sorry to hear of Teddy's loss."

"You have some reason to doubt whether Teddy killed himself?" She couldn't understand that one.

"It was Teddy's gun. I guess he killed himself. I don't know why he would. But — well, sometimes a person feels like there's no escape from their pain."

There was no fright in Marilyn's face now. It had disappeared. She was rather composed. I wondered if she might be relieved that Teddy was dead.

"I don't know if I can face the police alone," she said hesitantly.

"Call your mother," I said. "Then the police. Your mother can hold your hand while you give the police your story."

She bristled stiffly. "Oh, I get it. No client, no money. So, you think you're so smart now." She smiled resentfully. "Well why don't you just string my mother along?" She got up and turned in a huff. "Sorry there's no fees in it for you. But I guess there's no repeat business once the client is dead."

I didn't answer her. No retort. Nothing. I just wanted her to leave. She went, and I had a metallic taste in my mouth. I tried to work on a couple of projects for the rest of the afternoon. But I wasn't productive.

A client came in to see Grant. I told Hildy I was through for the night and left. I walked into a crowded little restaurant and had a late dinner. Then I went home and to bed. No dreaming. At least none that I recall.

Teddy Noren's so-called suicide was on page six in the morning newspaper. There wasn't much to it. Young artist takes own life. Marilyn Riley was mentioned. She'd been his closest friend. The reporter who wrote the story hadn't connected her with Lloyd Henderson.

I read the paper on the way to my accounting office. Page one was a story about terrorist threats of bombing another government agency. Hildy tore off a sheet from a memo pad as I walked in the door. "Mr. Henderson called. He wants you to call him. ASAP. He's at his home."

In my office, I sat behind my gray Steelcase desk, and drank my usual cup of acidic coffee. I rang the number Hildy gave me. That voice was familiar. It was Paul Manfred. He transferred me to Henderson.

"Can you come right over, Dr. Cramer?"

"Something up?"

"Long Beach. Take the train." He could be demanding. "Paul will meet you at the station. He's patient, Dr. Cramer. He'll wait until you get there." End of conversation. *Click.*

There was a click. I don't like being ordered around like a puppet. I fumed for about 20 seconds and slammed the receiver down. Money. Money talks, money beckons. Greed, power ...

I went in to Grant's office and told him about Lloyd Henderson's call.

"Go and see him," Grant said. "Never keep a paying client waiting."

"I was afraid you might say that."

I caught a train from Penn Station. The conduit of a seemingly endless torrent of every imaginable type of human existence — and the late-night haunt of all the bizarre urban castoffs. The city's sad display case of tragic human pathology. I saw one person standing in front of a brick wall one time. Screaming his head off at it. I thought President Obama's costly government healthcare takeover would eliminate all these medical problems. I had hoped that I was through with the Hendersons and with the Rileys. What was it now?

Sure enough, Paul Manfred was waiting for me at the station in Long Beach. Leaning against the glossy fender of Henderson's armored, black stretch limo.

He nodded and held the rear door open for me. I climbed in. He seated himself behind the wheel. Power door locks cachunked shut, bulletproof power windows up, sealing the outside world into silence. I was pressed back into the leather seat as he pushed the gas pedal to the floor. Deep plush seats, expansive wood trimmed interior, TV, cell phone — what a life.

We followed the Long Island gold coast, then came into an isolated shoreline area. At one stretch of beach I saw a row of enormous dark boulders, rising out of the water like medieval stockade, then the beach house, or rather, beach mansion. It *was* sprawling. White and blue pillared Georgian colonial. Brick, with a lawn big enough to play football. A uniformed valet was waiting for us. He must have seen the car coming up the pebbled drive — or did some hidden security cameras tip him off to our arrival? I got out, and Paul drove the car around the house, probably to a garage in the back.

The valet took me through a gleaming, pink marble floored entrance hall, up a plush carpeted grand staircase, and knocked on a door with ivory trim. That voice barked, and the valet pushed the heavy brass door handle. I walked into a large room.

More thick carpets, impressionist paintings on the cherry paneled walls, a crimson velvet divan, and matching wing chairs. A sitting room? A study? What difference did it make? I was ready to move in. Luxury. Thick, rich, luxury. I could live like this.

There was a polished Chippendale desk, and behind it was King Lear himself. He motioned to a club chair. I sat down. He got up, walked deliberately to a sofa and sat down facing me.

Lloyd Henderson was wearing a navy-blue suit. Crisp white button-down shirt, French cuffs clasped with gold and pearl cuff links. There was no tie. Why would he need a tie? He took out an envelope from his left inside jacket pocket and handed it to me. I opened it and read it.

The note inside wasn't dated.

*Scandal is something we should all avoid. Keep Marilyn under control. $50,000 please. You'll hear from us again.*

I put the sheet back in the envelope and gave it back to Henderson. "When did you get this?" I asked. Of course, I had just put my fingerprints on the letter and envelope. Stupid. Was he trying to set me up?

"This morning."

"No idea what Marilyn was up to?"

"No idea," he said.

"Letter and envelope were typed. Someone could have done the typing at home, or in a computer store where word processors are on display. Or in a university library, a photocopy shop. The list is endless. What are you going to do now? You could just pay the fifty thousand, and whoever they are might go away. On the other hand, ..."

"Yes," he said. "It might be only the first payment."

"You could try a bluff. Don't pay and see what happens."

"I hate all kinds of uncontrolled publicity, especially if it's scandalous, Dr. Cramer," Lloyd Henderson said. "But I won't sit still for blackmail. And I won't have my granddaughter put in danger."

"What do you want *me* to do, Mr. Henderson?"

"You must have experience dealing with blackmail in your line of work."

"Not too often." I was thankful for that. "I try to avoid criminal expert witnessing."

"I want you to straighten this mess out. And *quietly.*"

"Who's my client? You or your daughter?"

"I am. You deal directly with me on this. As for my daughter, I want her out of the picture," he barked. "Marilyn gets this from *her,*" he practically spit the words out through his clenched teeth. "I resent my daughter, Dr. Cramer. She has always defied me."

"Well, I suppose there's some consolation," I said. "You have your other two daughters."

"Yes. Cora and Sandra. A man could not wish for two more loyal daughters."

"Uh huh."

"I had hopes for Marilyn. Don't ask me what she could have done to provoke this kind of blackmail threat."

I thought about the copy of Bellini's *Madonna* in Teddy Noren's apartment. Maybe he had something to do with fake paintings being sold through Myra's art gallery.

Now I'd have to see Marilyn again, and I wasn't looking forward to it. But it didn't look like I had much choice. At this point, she was the only lead I had. Did Marilyn have something to do with passing off forged paintings, or was there really a major art theft of some kind?

Lloyd Henderson rose to his feet. "You may as well join me for lunch, Dr. Cramer."

Lunch was in an enclosed patio, at the back of the mansion. A redwood table was set for four, with china, crystal, and sterling. A woman in a neat blue and white uniform brought platters of thick prime rib, and we helped ourselves. Henderson introduced me to his two daughters, Cora and Sandra. Both were elegantly dressed. Cora was the oldest, probably in her late 40s. Rather plain, with reddish brown hair. Sandra was the middle kid, with honey blond hair, high cheek bones, and strikingly attractive face. They smelled fine. After the introductions, Henderson started talking about his computer and information systems businesses.

From the back of the porch I saw the garage. The doors were open. It was big enough for five cars, and I could see a maintenance bay in it. Beyond it was a tennis court. Formal gardens, an Olympic sized swimming pool and, a white marble fountain. What a life.

"John Burton tells me you are an accountant—a bean counter."

"Yes, mostly management accounting."

"Are you a CPA then?"

"I'm a Certified Public Accountant, a Certified Management Accountant, and I have a Certified Financial Forensics credential and a CRFAC."

"What's a CRFAC?"

"Certified Forensic Accountant."

Henderson waved his fork and said, "Well, you might be interested in the new computerized manufacturing system we just installed in one of my plants. We're using an online process flow control system fully integrated with our work-in-process accounting system. We use embedded bar-code scanners and hand-held light pens to track work-in-process through every single stage of assembly."

"A paperless system," I inserted.

"Right. The system lowers my cost. Paper and pencils are replaced by bar code scanners, monitors, and flash memory chips. I can change the product mix at will, and we've cut investment in inventory by more than 50 percent. We have dozens of quality test points all along the production lines that feed corrective information back to the production machines, in real time. All our processes are automatically self-adjusting. If there's anything our robotic equipment can't correct immediately, a message is displayed on one of the monitors, and that machine halts until an engineer makes the correction."

"So, you get assembly and test information on demand—in real time," I said.

"Absolutely. It gives greater control over every phase of the operation. We've cut defects by using Six-Sigma at every level."

"Black belts, green belts," I said. Six-Sigma is a business management strategy that tries to improve the quality of process output by identifying and eliminating defects and errors. A process that is in control by one sigma, has about 68 percent of the product without defects. If it is at two sigma, 95 percent is without defects. By three sigma it is up to 99.7 percent. At six sigma, a company has virtually removed defects, which is an admirable goal. It's a registered service mark and trademark of Motorola, Inc.

"Yes, we have different belts," Henderson smiled.

"How many bar code tracking stations scan the work in process on the production line?"

"We track every single item of inventory from the time it leaves the supplier's shipping dock until the time it's sold to our customer. We scan bar codes when materials arrive in our receiving dock, when they are picked for production, at more than a hundred points along the production lines, and again when they are warehoused as finished products. We scan each item again when it's selected for sale to the customer."

"We give the warehouse workers a holster for their scanning guns. Some of them consider it quite a handsome little sidearm," he sniffed condescendingly, and smirked with the corner of his mouth. "They fancy themselves to be high-tech cowboys."

"*Total control* is the name of the game, Dr. Cramer. Knowledge is power that turns into money. I know exactly how much money I've got invested in inventory at every critical point — and I know exactly how much inventory is walking out the door in my employee's pockets as well. Believe me, we prosecute them to the hilt when we catch them stealing from me."

"We want materials to be delivered just-in-time (JIT) for production, and we want finished products coming off the line just-in-time for sale to our customers. In this business one day can mean millions of dollars in obsolete inventory. That is something I absolutely will not tolerate from my people. I don't need to tell you, I have good people — they keep inventories at the absolute minimum," he crowed with steely pride.

"I read last year in a *Financial Executive* report that there will be a number of major changes over the next few years. Widespread expansion of electronic banking, improved commercial applications of artificial intelligence, blockchain data, skyrocketing global connectivity, mass integration of corporate databases in supply chain management, and the ascension of the Chief Information Officer into the executive suite," I said. Henderson seemed to be enjoying the conversation.

"I teach my students about lean accounting, which organizes costs according to the value chain and collects both financial and nonfinancial information by focusing on the elimination of waste. Accounting measures are being designed to motivate the employees and management to create customer value."

"Good for you," Henderson replied.

After the rich, if heavy, meal, Paul Manfred drove me back to the train station. Not one word passed between us.

When I got back to Grand Central, I decided to walk the 10 blocks to my accounting office. Walking is boring, for sure, but I can think about problems and help depreciate my Fitbit. Hildy was on the phone when I arrived, so I waited for her to finish. "Is Tom around?"

"Yes," she said, "Want me to buzz his office?"

"Thanks."

Tom Reardon walked into my office a few minutes later. He was a tall Irish redhead with penetrating eyes and large Adam's apple. After graduating with a degree in accounting, he'd worked for the FBI as a Special Agent for ten years, investigating white-collar financial crimes.

He sat down in the chair across from my desk and I said, "See if you can get a line on a Paul Manfred. He acts as the bodyguard for Lloyd Henderson — one of our new clients. Mid-to-late 20s, tall, solid build, brown hair. There's a good chance he has a police record."

"Is this okay with John?"

"Sure, we have a paying client."

I gave him some information about Marilyn and Myra Riley, the death of Teddy Noren, the maybe theft Myra told me about, and the blackmail letter to Lloyd Henderson.

Tom said, "Will do," and went on his way. I called Marilyn's apartment. She was there. "Are you staying there?"

"Yes," she said. "It's awful, but where am I supposed to go?"

"Nowhere, I guess. I'll be right over."

"Why? I thought you were finished with me."

"No such luck." I hung up. The manners of a forensic investigator.

# Five

*Those who listen to the siren song of the brokers of art as an investment, should keep in mind and cast an exceedingly wary look in the direction of the salesroom commentators whose enthusiasm grows even more round-eyed as the price mounts.*

—Gerald Reitlingers

I didn't expect Marilyn to be cordial, and she wasn't. She lounged in a rocking chair, one leg tossed over the other. She was wearing a loose sweater and black stretch pants. Her feet were bare.

"It's your grandfather," I said, sitting down. "He got a letter today. A blackmail letter."

She was surprised, or she pretended to be. "What's that got to do with me?"

I repeated the contents of the letter to her, word for word. "Your grandfather asked me to look into it." I looked at her, waited for a reply.

When there wasn't any, I said, "This is no joke. I want you to be straight with me. What do you know about Teddy's death?"

"Nothing," she said testily.

"No forgeries of famous art works, or anything like that?"

Silence.

"You'd like to help your grandfather, wouldn't you?"

Her frown soured. "Yeah. Like he helped my mother. He kicked her out."

"I thought he liked you. Your mother told me he did."

"I'm his only grandchild," she peered at me.

I said, "How come Cora and Sandra never got married and started families?"

"My grandfather wanted them to stay home and take care of him. I guess he's afraid of dying a miserable, lonely old man. And who'd want to marry Cora? She's got no life. Sandra has some potential. Or she did have. But, she chose to stick with grandpa. I guess they're both kinda afraid of him — or of being disinherited."

"Where were you yesterday when Teddy was doing his swan song?"

"Working."

"At the art gallery?"

"No. Posing."

"For who?"

"Frank Masters. Like auntie used to say, I'm popular with the artists. They like what they see."

"Why did an artist own a gun?"

"Maybe it made him feel more like a man," she said. "Teddy wasn't a strong person."

Her answer seemed clearly evasive to me. I left it alone. "I'd like to talk to this guy Frank Masters."

"I can give you his address. I've got nothing to hide. I'll do what I can to cooperate with you, Mr. Cramer." Her voice now had a saccharine sweetness.

"The other guy you mentioned — Bram Walker — the one who paints landscapes. How can I get in touch with him?"

"I'll give you his address too. Anything else you'd like to know? How about Judy Chicago? Oh, I guess you wouldn't know her."

"I know who Judy Chicago is."

"Oh?"

"And O'Keefe, Rivers, Gorman. I don't live in a cubicle, Marilyn. I've heard of Picasso — have you ever heard of Luca Pacioli?"

"Nope. Who is he? He's not Renaissance."

I smiled, teasing. "Pacioli was a contemporary of Leonardo da Vinci. A Franciscan monk. He's considered to be the father of accounting. Wrote a book on mathematics, and double-entry accounting. You're a bookkeeper, aren't you?"

"Cute," she said with a snit. Then she smiled, slightly, with a pinprick of amusement in her eyes. "I suppose I could learn to tolerate you, if you weren't so obnoxious."

"Me? I'm the easiest accounting professor in the world." I got up, stretched, and took a walk through her apartment. She got up quickly and followed right behind me. I went into the room where I'd seen the two digital scales earlier. They were gone. So was the wax.

Her finger nails bit into my arm. Her face was ugly this time. "What do you think you're doing? What are you looking for?" she snapped.

"Two laboratory scales."

She seemed to develop a harder time breathing suddenly. "I don't know what you're talking about."

"What kind of trouble are you in Marilyn? Are you stealing from the art gallery to pay for drugs?"

She released her grip from my arm. Her face was stiff. "You're crazy. Look, you can't just come in here —"

"Listen to how this sounds," I snapped. "Before you came to my office you tipped somebody off. They came here and took the two scales you were using to weigh crack cocaine. Didn't they? Then you went back and called the police. But when they arrived, there are no scales, no crack, and no wax. You're involved with fake paintings aren't you. So fake that some blackmailer is using the information to put a bite on your grandfather — with or without your help."

She backed away, frightened this time. "You can't prove that. You can't even prove there ever were any scales here. And you won't go to the police. You can't tell them you were here, and saw two scales, and didn't report a dead body. You're a CPA. Maybe they'll think *you* did it. You know the law. They'll pull your license for good."

"Do you hate your grandfather that much?"

"No. I—I—" That threw her a little bone. Then she went to the cream-colored couch and sat down. Her hands gripped her knees. Her knuckles were white. "I had no idea — I couldn't blackmail anyone. You just don't understand. I, I—"

I stood over her. "Tell me what happened, Marilyn. Tell me everything. I'm listening."

She looked up at me with wet eyes. So, the kid could cry. She wasn't such a hard-boiled brat after all.

"Teddy and I needed money. The things I posed for never got into any catalogs or magazines. But we never sold anything real — it was only wax. Some art dealers. They wanted crack … and…. But I don't know anything about forged paintings. I didn't take any money from the gallery."

"I get the picture." Small-time drug dealers sometimes passed off chunks of wax for crack. Buyers can't tell the difference until someone tries to smoke it. "You must not have been doing it for long. Who came here and picked up the scales?"

"Bram," she almost whispered.

"Why did you and Teddy need the money? You both have jobs."

"Yeah. Minimum wage, right," she huffed.

"Did Teddy ever argue with Bram Walker or Frank Masters?"

The question puzzled her. "No. Why should they argue? What do you mean?"

"Were you cheating on Teddy with Frank or Bram?"

"No, I wasn't. That's ridiculous."

I walked to the painting on the easel. "Who painted this?"

"Teddy."

"Could Frank or Bram copy his style?"

"I guess so. Why?" She didn't understand my questioning. "Sometimes they would copy each other for fun. I don't get it. What are you saying?"

"This painting's an oil. It's a copy. Teddy used acrylics, didn't he?"

Maybe it was what I said, or the way I said it — she jumped up and scrutinized the painting. "It *is* an oil." She faced me, some of the cocky arrogance wiped out. "What's going on? You're not telling me something." She turned suddenly on me, clenched her fists and started banging her knuckles into my chest. "What is going on?" She demanded.

I grabbed her wrists, "Teddy didn't paint this forgery. It was somebody else, wasn't it? Why? I don't know. But I don't think Teddy was alone when he was killed."

That caught her. Her chest heaved and fell, as she reeled in confusion. "Y — You think he was murdered? That's crazy. Why would someone stop to paint a picture?"

"I don't know Marilyn. But whoever it was brought their own paint. Oil paint. Look at this, linseed oil — Teddy wouldn't have used oil with acrylics.

I think somebody killed Teddy—before or after they did the painting. Teddy knew artists who could copy his style."

"Bram? Frank? No. No way. We were all good friends. They were Teddy's friends as much as mine. Look, Bram did some cutting. Frank never knew anything about our dealing. But why kill Teddy? There's no reason for either of them to kill Teddy."

"Maybe I'm wrong. I've been wrong lots of times before. But the suicide— it just doesn't add up."

She slumped into a chair. "This is just crazy." She looked up at me. "Why didn't you tell the cops?"

"What, tell them my suspicions? What do I have as evidence? A painting done in oil. If it was murder—how does that tie into the blackmail? I have no theory at this point. There's nothing so practical as a good theory. Maybe you can tell *me* some of the answers."

"You're the investigator—uh, accountant—or whatever you are. You tell me."

"I wish I could, Marilyn," I said as I let out a breath. I didn't want to scare her. But I couldn't help adding, "Can't you see the danger you might be in? Your boyfriend's dead, and your grandfather gets a blackmail threat. Someone wants you under control. Under control about what? The police will love that one. And the media—I can see the headlines now. Money, drugs ... murder, blackmail, scandal. Your grandfather's news. Rich as Midas. The media will have a feeding frenzy over it."

"What are you gonna do?" She seemed cautious this time.

"Talk to Frank and Bram. You'll help, won't you?"

She talked through her teeth. "I said I would."

"Well, why don't you give me their addresses and phone numbers." I gave her a business card, and she wrote on the back of it.

"They don't have to talk to you, you know," she pointed out. "You should probably take me with you."

"They'll think you turned on them."

"I don't care," she said. Resigned, almost irritated.

Bram Walker didn't live far from Marilyn. A three-story row house, with worn-out granite steps, leading up to a weather beaten front door. It was an old building, but in decent repair. Bram lived in a third-floor walkup. An attractive girl with olive skin opened the door. Her eyes focused on Marilyn, and I saw the daggers in them.

"Is Bram Walker here?" I asked.

"Yes," the girl said, looking me over warily.

We walked into the room, and Marilyn introduced me to Nadja. She was tall, slim, with wavy black hair, and olive skin. She was wearing a floor length bath robe.

The front room was small, with a plaid couch and two chairs. There was a bookcase full of paperbacks, a low table with a brass ashtray on it, and a hard cover book about surrealism. While Nadja went to get Bram Walker, I picked up the book from the table. I opened it to an illustration of a painting by Hans Arp. I flipped through the pages and admired some works by Rene Magritte. Could you forge paintings from these pictures? Not likely; you'd need to see the original.

Bram Walker strode in, bare chested. Short pants, with no belt. His feet were bare. He was tall and almost emaciated, with dark brown hair. About 25. There was a half-inch scar at the corner of his mouth. He invited us to sit down. Nadja hadn't come out with him.

We all sat down, chummy like. A little hokey. Marilyn gave the introductions. Bram smiled, politely.

"Mr. Cramer is an accountant," Marilyn explained. "He's working for my grandfather. He — uh — wants to ask you a couple of questions."

His eyebrows rose, and his lips thinned. "Questions? About what?"

"Teddy Noren," I said.

"Teddy? What a drag. He was a good friend of mine."

"You were supposed to meet him before lunch yesterday?" I said.

"Yeah. In the Village. But he never showed."

"No. He was dead. Did you try to call him, when he didn't show?"

"Yeah. There was no answer."

"What did you do then?"

"I went home and worked on a painting."

"Until Marilyn called you to get two scales, and a block of wax from her apartment?"

He stiffened, turned slowly to Marilyn, and glowered. His face was ugly. "Marilyn talks too much." He turned back to me and smiled like a strung-out cobra. "What does an accountant have to do with this anyway? I don't have to talk to you."

"You mean you'd rather talk to the police?" Sometimes that line worked; sometimes it didn't.

He smiled blandly. "Do you think the police would care about the ravings of a manic-depressive, grade-B model?"

Marilyn was cut and angry. "Bram! You can't talk about me like that. My grandfather's being blackmailed ..."

His smile floated toward Marilyn. "I thought you didn't care about your moneybag's grandfather."

"Why did you say manic-depressive?" I asked. I was beginning not to care for Mr. Bram Walker. I was crossing him off my Christmas list.

"Well the dear child has peaks and fits of depression," he said to me. "She had a nervous breakdown once. One time at a party—"

"Never mind," I growled. "I was hoping you might be willing to cooperate. I'm not the police, but I know a couple of detectives who'd be very interested in your drug business."

"Look, I told you—"

"I think the police would be very interested in the fact you went to Teddy's apartment, killed him, did a forgery with your own paint—"

His face chalked. "Killed him? What are you talking about? Teddy committed suicide."

"That's what I said."

"I didn't kill Teddy." He shot a glance at his long, paint stained fingers. "You can't accuse me. Teddy was dead when I got there. That's the truth. I saw it was suicide, and I left."

"You admit you were there?"

"Yeah, yeah." He started to squirm a little. He looked at Marilyn. "I'm sorry about Teddy, Marilyn. Honest. He was a real friend. If somebody murdered him, it surely wasn't me." He looked at me. "You can't blame me for saying I wasn't there, can you? Who wants to get in the middle of something like that?"

"You're telling the truth now." I didn't think *I* wanted to be in the middle of it either.

"It looked like suicide—but murder—well, if I can help you—I won't slow you down. I don't really know if it helps, but I was there. When Teddy didn't show for lunch, I called him. There was no answer. So, I went up to his apartment. His door was open. So, I went in. I saw he was dead. I was scared, so I just left."

"Why didn't you take the scales then?" I wanted to know.

"I didn't think of it. I was scared. I just wanted to get out of there. Then when Marilyn called, and told me I better go get the scales before the cops showed up — well, I went over and took them. I was scared- to- death the whole time that somebody would catch me there. I imagined the cops walking in and thinking I did it."

"Did you bring your own paints with you?"

"No. What would I do that for?"

I told him about the oil painting on the easel, and Teddy Noren only working with acrylic.

"That's weird. He never used oils," he sighed. "He never knew the joys of melding texture and color." He looked at me with a hollow grin. "I guess you wouldn't understand."

"I know enough." A stretched canvas must be painted with a whitewash coat, before the artist starts to paint. They usually wait for the canvas to dry, before painting. But some artists don't wait for the canvas to dry. They start painting while the canvas is still wet. That way they can push the paint around in bold strokes, as they swipe with pallet knives and brushes. In case they don't like what, they've painted, they can change it. It's called painting wet-on-wet.

"Are you a weekend artist?" he asked.

"I was, but I gave it all up. I did a year of sketches and drawings, and some painting. I was never very good, so I gave it up for the exciting life of an accounting professor."

"So, you're a professor? They get paid more than artists. If you laid out all accountants end-to-end, it'll probably be a good thing." His head sort of dropped to one side.

"I've heard that about economists and lawyers." I broke it off. "Look, I didn't come here to talk about — "

He waved a hand. "All right. Never mind. I can go on endlessly about art."

"Well, I can't. Do you have the two scales here?"

"No. Look around, if you want."

"Where did you put them?"

"Sorry. I'm not going to tell you that one."

Nadja walked in. "When do we go back to work?" she said.

Bram Walker stood up. "Sorry I can't be any more help." It was clearly a brush off.

Marilyn and I left.

Outside, she asked, "You hungry?" Meaning *she* was hungry.

We found a place where they served Thai food. As we ate, I said, "Nadja doesn't like you much, does she?"

"I'm a more popular model than she is."

There was steamed rice, under my intensely hot curried chicken. "Okay. Now tell me the real reason."

"She thinks I took Teddy away from her," Marilyn huffed. "Teddy never had any real interest in her."

"Does Nadja stay with Bram?"

"She has to live somewhere," Marilyn said, as if logical. She drank some Coke. "Bram will dump her as soon as he gets tired of her."

I sipped my virgin Piña Colada. I got hooked on 'em when I was at an accounting convention in Hawaii.

* * *

Frank Masters lived in the Village. Bleeker Street. It was a decent apartment building, with an onyx-walled lobby. The building had three wooden benches near the two elevators. There was a "No Smoking" sign in the elevator.

The elevator took us up to the seventh floor, and we walked down the corridor on clean, maroon and gray carpet. Masters opened the door for us. "Hi, Marilyn. Who's this?"

He was in about his upper 20s, swarthy. With a thin mustache, and black hair, brushed straight back. Marilyn introduced me, and we walked into his living room. Spacious for a New York apartment.

The living room was furnished with a glass-topped cocktail table in front of a long white sofa, with two-winged back chairs on either side of the sofa. There was an oriental rug on the floor. Paintings covered most of the walls.

Masters was casual. He wore a light blue open collar shirt, khaki pants, and what looked like worn Dockers on his feet. He didn't have on any socks.

"I am sorry about Teddy," he said gently to Marilyn. He looked at me with a faint smile. "And how can I help you?"

"I'm looking into some issues related to the death of Teddy Noren."

"Police?"

"Nope. Just helping a friend. I'm working for Marilyn's grandfather."

"Ahh, the mighty Lloyd Henderson." He said it without relish. "I despise the filth rich. Jealousy, I am afraid."

"Did you see Teddy Noren yesterday?"

"No."

"You had no contact with him at all yesterday?"

"No."

"You and Teddy were good friends, weren't you?"

"Yeah. The best."

"Do you know if he had any enemies?"

"Enemies? Teddy? None that *I* know of."

"I think Teddy was murdered, Frank."

There was a surprising look of emotion in his face, and in his voice. "I heard it was suicide."

"Somebody did an oil painting in his apartment, either before killing him, or after."

"Why would someone do that?"

"I don't know. It was a copy of Bellini's *Madonna*."

"That's weird," he mused. "I don't like talking about death. Murder or a suicide. The idea is about as unappealing to me as cold grits."

"You didn't see Teddy yesterday. Did you see Bram Walker at all?"

"Yeah. We had dinner together."

"Do you know about Bram's sideline?"

He looked bored. "Sideline?" he quizzed. "No."

"Crack cocaine? Faked paintings?"

The glance he shot at Marilyn said, 'you talk too much.' "Mr. Accountant, I am afraid I've got a lot of work to do. If you don't mind, I need to get back to it."

I was getting another brush-off. Marilyn and I stood up, and I thanked Masters for his time. Then we walked out. Forensic accountants don't have subpoena powers, but we also don't have to give Miranda rights.

"What now?" she said, when we were on the sidewalk.

"Well, I'm going to take you home. If you get any invitations from Frank or Bram, I suggest you forget it. Just stay home."

That didn't settle too well with her. "I hate staying there. You think I'm in danger?"

"Neither one of them were happy you talked to me. And somebody is selling fake paintings that nobody wants to talk about."

"But these guys are my friends."

"Choir boys don't traffic in the kind of drugs you were dealing, Marilyn. And you don't know who might have been fronting the money for it. Besides, when you cut bags of crack with rocks made from wax, somebody is liable to get really unhappy. Use your head. Listen to my advice."

Diluting a product with cheap materials causes what is known as a *favorable material mix* variance. But the quality of the product will suffer if it's done too much—like Marilyn's crack. That's why both favorable and unfavorable variances need to be interpreted with a clear understanding of the facts. Hospitals measure patient mix, a similar concept. Some illness treatments are more profitable than others. An abnormal inflow of patients who need low margin treatments will cause an unfavorable patient (sales) mix variance and reduce overall profitability of the hospital.

There was a taxi station nearby with two yellow cabs waiting. We climbed into the first one. I gave the driver Marilyn's address. This drive would probably be a low margin trip for the driver—lowering his sales mix variance for the day. So, the second taxi was left waiting there, with the driver watching the sales quantity variance go down. I guess low margin trips are better than no trips.

Shortly we pulled up to Marilyn's dingy brick building.

"What if I get hungry?" she asked.

"Have some Chinese food sent up to you and stay inside with your door locked."

Her fingers were on my wrist. "You'll call me later, won't you?"

"I'll check with you tonight. And tomorrow morning." Going back to that apartment was probably not easy. I didn't blame her.

# Six

*Management accountants have been so involved in the details of the traditional cost accounting system that they are not aware of the 'big picture' changes that have occurred in cost structure and behavior.*

—Thomas B. Lammert and Robert Ehrsam

Tom Reardon was sitting across from me in my sixth floor, small Columbia University office in Uris Hall. He was sitting peacefully, with his long legs stretched out. I stepped over his big feet to get my Henderson file, and sat behind my desk again. It was late in the day. "You look as happy as a tornado in a trailer park," I said.

"Paul Manfred," he said with a grin, but it was not a pleasant smile. "Did some time for manslaughter. A rough character. He got off easy. Plea bargain, you know how it goes."

I gave him Frank Masters's address. Then I described Bram Walker. I wanted to know if someone of that description might have been seen going into Masters's building, lugging two laboratory scales. "That would be anytime yesterday. There's a taxi stand near the building. Maybe talk to the cab drivers; one of them might have seen him." Then I gave him everything I had on Henderson, the blackmail, Teddy Noren, the Rileys, and the two sisters who still stayed with their daddy.

"Paul Manfred might be involved with the blackmail thing," Tom said.

"I'm not going to overlook that angle. And while you're at Masters' apartment, check to see if there's a service entrance. Bram might have gone through there with the two scales."

51

"Anything else, boss?"

"I need you to get over to Myra Riley's art gallery. Check her accounting records. See if you find any evidence of Marilyn cooking the books. Look for anything that might suggest of money laundering. See if the cost of artwork sold is overstated in any way. Did they pay a fair price for the artwork they bought and then sold? We are trying to determine if fake paintings are being sold. What is their gross margin on sales? Look for any related shell, dummy, or facade entities. Are there any sales not supported by consignment slips — you know, the usual routine. Not likely they have any internal controls. But keep your eyes open for any compliance problems with whatever controls they might have."

The redheaded Irishman left, and I moved to my easy chair. I started going through some of my backlogged reading material. Under the pile of journals and technical pronouncements, I found my old AICPA booklet on internal control systems. It was published back in the 1970s. But, I keep it around, and refer to it often. It's based on a manual accounting system for a manufacturing company. It has great diagrams of paperwork flows for every major cycle in a business: sales and receivables, purchasing and inventory, billing and collections, payroll, accounts payable, you name it. The whole business process. It's good for understanding the basic principles of checks and balances. I must've put it in my reading pile to make some slides or handouts for class. The Public Company Accounting Oversight Board or PCAOB now requires external auditors to do walkthroughs of internal control, especially for risk assessments. Auditors are also now required to test and issue an opinion on these internal controls.

In today's electronic environment, where customers and suppliers exchange paperless electronic purchase orders and invoices, it never ceases to amaze me how many organizations still use old, outmoded accounting information systems (AIS). I don't know how they survive doing business like that.

Bob Kaplan at Harvard thinks they won't, especially with the competition in today's global economy. He wrote a book years ago on the rise and fall of managerial accounting, and how outmoded accounting systems — that spread costs over products, like oil paint with a palette knife, result in inaccurate product cost determinations and uncompetitive pricing policies. He advocates a system of Activity Based Costing (ABC).

ABC says that managers should identify the specific activities that drive costs. These are known, not surprisingly, as "*cost-drivers*." This phrase is one of the creative labels we use in accounting. Accurate identification of the salient cost drivers for a product allows managers to calculate, in greater detail, how costs will vary with the specific activities that drive production costs up or down. Once this calculation is done, refined and detailed application of costs to products can be made, based on how many cost drivers are relevant to a specific product. This technique gives both a more accurate product cost calculation, and a more accurate basis upon which to form product pricing strategies.

I agreed with him on that score. And with today's computing power, the cost/benefit ratio for detailed information systems gets lower every day, allowing more accurate cost accounting systems to be implemented, at lower processing cost for most companies.

While I was flipping through some of the journals in the pile, I spotted in *Cost Management Systems: A Digest of the Relevant Literature*, a short review of "Pitfalls in Evaluating Risky Projects." The authors, Hodder and Riggs in the *Harvard Business Review*, argued that discounted cash flow procedures are not inherently biased against long-term investment. But managers need to set realistic hurdle rates, and carefully examine their own assumptions. Well, they're not kidding.

Skimming an issue of *Strategic Finance*, I read a piece by Ir-Woon Kim and Irjan T. Sadhwani titled, "Is Your Inventory Really All There?" They indicated that "most inventory discrepancies in manufacturing companies are due to employee, vendor, and customer errors, rather than theft." Add that to employee theft — there's errors, and then sometimes there's "errors."

Well I certainly disagree with that. There is at least one trillion dollars' worth of fraud in the U.S. annually. In the U. S., employees out steal shoplifters.

There was no letter from *Strategic Finance* accepting my article about sunk costs. Oh well, it was only a practitioner-type article which did not count as an A-type journal. Only extremely esoteric articles count in today's academic life. If the article was practical and worthwhile, zero credit is often given to the professor. The life of a research professor.

I picked up a piece by Anna Miller writing about an Advancing Government Accountability (AGA) research study entitled "Managerial Cost Accounting in the Federal Government: Providing Useful Information for Decision Making." I needed to add some of this material in my classroom.

It always amazed me that there are thousands of articles written by accounting and finance professors on earnings management (or cooking the books) for private businesses, but little is written about cooking the governmental books. It happens every day, but accounting professors ignore it.

Even before quasi-governmental Fannie Mae and Freddie Mac destroyed the world's economy in 2009, they were engaged in "wrong way earnings management." They were caught pushing much of their income into the future because they thought interest rates were going up. They were trying to smooth their earnings.

Next, I read a stack of newsletters: *The Art Newsletter*, *The ART News*, and *Art Times*. In *Art in America*, I saw that a painting by Amedeo Modigliani of a nude female sold for $157.2 million. I flipped through the latest issue of *Arts Editor* and fell asleep in the recliner reading *Apollo*. *Art and Action* was unopened on the floor in front of me when I woke up from a bad dream.

I dreamed I was chairing a meeting of the Federal Cost Accounting Standards Board. The CASB issues accounting standards for virtually all federal government-negotiated contracts of $650,000 or more. I was addressing the distinguished group.

"A *static budget* provides cost and revenue estimates for one level of activity. Conversely, a *flexible budget* (also known as a dynamic budget) is prepared for more than one level of activity (*i.e.*, 13,000, 14,000, or 15,000 units of production). The reason for preparing budgets for various levels of activity is to provide managers with information about costs over a range of production activity, since the actual level may be different from the expected level."

At that moment, Professor Glenn A. Welsch stepped out from his oil painting on the wall. He raised his fist and shouted, "The Just-in-Time theory of manufacturing brings raw materials and production together to eliminate waste." Then he pulled a high-powered Uzi water pistol out from under his suit coat, and blasted Professor Charles Horngren with Chartreuse acrylic paint.

As Horngren was dropping to the floor mortally wounded, on his last gasp he wheezed, "Cost accounting is the major obstacle for making U.S. manufacturing companies competitive. The JIT philosophy treats work-in process inventory as a liability rather than an asset. So, management can't use a large work-in-process account as a cushion." Then in a hiss of steam, Horngren dissolved into a pool of acrylic paint on the floor. He was replaced by a book entitled *Just-in-Time Accounting* by Steven M. Bragg. What a world.

Just then M. Suzanne Oliver walked into the room. She strode to the podium where I was standing, seized the microphone, and began lecturing.

"A cost is relevant to decision making only if it will change depending upon the decision. That is, the cost will make a difference in the decision process, and, thus it is considered a *differential cost*. If a given cost will not change no matter what we decide, it is not relevant. A classic example is money spent in the past on mechanical repairs to a company's fleet of trucks. That cost will not change regardless of whether we decide to make another round of repairs or not. It's a *sunk cost*. The only effect it has on the decision to incur further repair costs is in estimating the potential benefits to be gained from the new repairs. The previous repair may, or may not, interact with the new repairs in enabling the company to gain more mileage use from the truck fleet."

Just then everyone seated at the long table reached into their jacket pockets, took out little toy Matchbox trucks and began racing them over the mirrored surface of the table—crashing them into each other, and making adolescent noises that sounded distinctly like, "vroom, vroom, errrrrrr ... crash!" It was a nightmarish scene.

To distract myself from the reversionary madness that had taken the committee members captive, I pulled my old intermediate financial accounting book out of my briefcase. I turned to the end of the chapter on cash and started working a four-column cash-proof, like it was a numeric Sudoku puzzle. It was for entertainment. Something I've always found relaxing. But this time it just didn't seem to help. I kept asking myself, "What about the U.S. $114 trillion unfunded liability?"

Glen Welsch was quickly subsumed back into his portrait on the wall, as if he was sucked in by a vacuum. Surrealistic accounting, I mused. Intriguing notion. Guess that's what governments have been doing for years—like taking the half billion-dollar savings and loan bailout "off-budget" to magically reduce the federal deficit. Surreal. Wonder if the bank would let me take my mortgage "off budget" when I apply for a personal loan? Think of the slight-of-hand gimmicks that the Democrat-controlled Congress used in 2010 to pass the health care reform bill.

The Congressional Budget Office (CBO) is the primary agency charged with reviewing congressional budgets and other legislative initiatives with budgetary implications. If private companies kept their records like the government does, their executives would all be in prison. Guess the joke is on us!

Budgeting is supposed to force us to take a hard, realistic look at our grandiose plans, and put them in cold hard dollars and cents. If the numbers don't add up, whether we like it or not, we'll need to adjust our plans to something that's more realistic. The problem is personalities. Dominant corporate visionaries are hard to reign-in, without formal control procedures on the budgetary process.

Then there's gaming. Middle managers pad their budget estimates with budgetary slack, because they know top management will cut the budget, and middle managers know how much they need to operate their departments. Top managers cut the budget because they know middle managers are padding the estimates. Seems stupid when you think about it.

Games. Some management accounting games get nasty, really fast. Like the receivables/payables game. Everyone wants to accelerate collection of their receivables, and delay payment of their payables. Great way to off-load your debt onto the other guy's balance sheet—just drag out your account payments, and he'll be forced to lean on his lines of credit to cover the cash shortage. If you're big enough, and he's small enough, he'll pile on enough debt financing to put himself in trouble. Then enters a "friend." He'll approach the little guy and offer to buy out the financially distressed company—at a steep discount, of course. If the mark sells out, the friend turns around and resells the little company to the big outfit. They just scooped it from the little guy for a song and dance—and he financed their cash payment for them.

I helped a small businessperson once who saw it coming. His biggest customer owed him $4,000,000. But he knew his own limits and wasn't about to be bullied by anyone. Losing their account wasn't as bad as losing his whole company. So, he got tough with them. "Pay the account, or I'll shut you off." And he meant it. They puffed back at him, "You can't shut us off. Nobody shuts us off. You shut us off, and you'll never do business with us again." After all, they were one of the biggest retailers in the industry—and his biggest customer. He shot back, "Watch me."

He shut them off—cut off all shipments of his product. They paid the $4,000,000. Why? He was supplying a quality product they were making money on reselling. They didn't want to lose him as a supplier. And he won their respect as a tough businessperson. We would have done a cash flow analysis and figured out he could have risked losing the $4,000,000. It would've hurt him, but he could absorb it. A big customer who doesn't pay, isn't a good customer, no matter how much product they order. Funny we don't teach more on this in B-schools. Might help save our students millions of bucks someday.

Then there's sheer politics. Like the government clerk who keeps putting a contractor's payment vouchers on the bottom of his in-basket pile, until the contractor takes him out to lunch and remembers the clerk's birthday with an envelope full of cash. It's amazing how fast government paperwork seems to get processed by that kind of jerk, oh, I mean clerk.

I floated in my dream to a ritzy restaurant lounge in Chicago. There he was, small time state government engineer, in one of his $2,500, custom tailored, black silk Brooks Brothers suits—half stewed. "Lenny," his alcohol reeking breath exuded rancid oil. "Why don't you smarten up, and join us?" He ran his fingers disdainfully up and down my gray Joseph A. Banks suit lapel. "Then you could be wearing suits like mine."

"I like my suits just fine," I shot back. Sniveling wretch. Would sell his own grandmother for a lousy chance to shakedown another small-time city contractor.

Government contractors. That's what the CASB is all about. Can't let contractors dump all their unrelated, underapplied overhead onto their cost-plus government contracts. The ones where companies are reimbursed for their production costs plus a predefined profit. Under the government's cost-plus contracting system, government contractors have an economic incentive to increase costs of production since they will be reimbursed — *i.e.,* add employees to the payroll, spare no expense on production, and lavish perquisites for managers and customers. More subtle manipulations also take place when costs associated with production that is unrelated to a government contract are shifted onto the government contract for reimbursement, through skewed overhead allocation formulas.

For example, the costs of building a new type of stealth bomber might be primarily driven by direct engineering hours since the product is unique. On the other hand, the costs of building a commercial jetliner might be primarily driven by direct labor hours, since the engineering problems and designs are better understood and more standardized. Therefore, by using direct engineering hours as the allocation basis for applying overhead to both contracts, a disproportionately large amount of overhead will be assigned to the stealth bomber — and will be reimbursed by the defense agency. The commercial jetliner will be charged with less overhead and will provide a more profitable sale to an airline. So, the government will be unwillingly subsidizing the costs and profitability of commercial production activities.

That's a main reason the CASB devoted a lot of attention to overhead allocation rules. Then they got defunded by Congress in September 1980. Four years later the Federal Acquisition Regulations (FAR) became effective and codified the CASB rules. CASB was refunded back in 1988. Now their rules extend beyond just the original domain of defense contracts, to all kinds of federal government contracts.

The lounge waffled and began to fade. The shadowy figure of a woman was walking toward me.

As I began to wake from my nightmare, the department secretary was approaching my office. It was morning. I must have been out the whole night. "There's a lady outside. Myra Riley."

"Escort the lady into my parlor," I said groggily, starting to sit up.

Myra Riley was wearing a knit pink dress, with some flowers on it.

"I thought I would hear from you." As my thoughts began to get clearer, I brought her up to date on the blackmail threat.

"You think it's because of the theft?" she said.

"Marilyn says she didn't steal anything."

"I'm so confused."

"Join the club."

"I'm glad my father kept you on to help us."

"I'll muddle my way through somehow." Then I told her why I thought Teddy was murdered. It shook her a bit. She wanted to know if I thought Marilyn was involved. I told her I didn't think so.

"There were two laboratory scales in Marilyn's apartment. There was a forged painting. I saw them when I found Teddy's body. While your daughter was in my office, the scales disappeared from the apartment."

"But—"

"I think Marilyn did her dealing out of her own apartment."

"Dealing?"

"Crack, cocaine. Or cut crack, so she tells me. She was passing off chunks of wax for the real thing. A risky game. Maybe some fakes of valuable paintings too."

That seemed to shake her as much as the thought that Teddy might have been murdered. "I think Marilyn's telling the truth at this point. I think she is feeling embarrassed and scared. She went with me to meet two of Teddy's friends. They weren't happy she was talking to me. One of them—Bram Walker, took the scales. The other one, Frank Masters, might be involved too."

"You think they're the ones who are trying to blackmail my father?"

"They have some leverage," I said.

"You'll stop them, won't you?" She reached across my desk and touched my hand, her eyes pleading.

"I guess that's what they're paying me for."

"Marilyn was without a father for too many years," she said. Her fingers were digging into my hand. "And I was without a husband. It hasn't been easy, Lenny."

We went outside. The air was cool, even if it did smell like grime, and the ceaseless carbon monoxide. "Shall I drop you off?" I said, waving at a cab.

"If you have other plans ..."

"I'm a working professor don't forget."

The cab stopped for us. I opened the door for her, and we got in. I slammed the door and gave the driver Myra's address. She sat by the far door and stared at me wistfully.

"Do you work 24 hours a day?" she asked from the blurry dusk.

"I'm a night owl."

We talked for a while as the cabby drove. It started to drizzle. Urban rain. April was like that. When we got to her place the temperature was lower. Myra got out, and I watched her go up the stairs to her apartment.

I stopped at my apartment to shave and check the mail, and then went to my accounting office. Tom was already there. "No cabby saw Walker go into Masters' apartment building," he reported. "And there's a service door in the back. Want me to look at Masters' apartment?"

"I can't ask you to do that. Don't get caught."

"Who, me?"

"If you happen to be in there legally, look for pipes, scales, chunks of wax—any signs of a small-time crack cutting operation. Check to see if there's any forged paintings."

"Do I take anything?"

"No. I don't want Masters to know anyone's been there. He probably won't keep any incriminating stuff in his apartment now anyway. And don't forget to check the financial records at the art gallery."

"I'll give the place a good shakedown legally, don't worry." Tom went away, and I got hold of Hildy. "Would you order me a Dr. Pepper and a ham sandwich, Hildy. Maybe a Danish."

"You'll get fat."

"A cheese Danish, with lots of sugar on it."

"I'll order something for myself," she said perkily. "Your treat. You've been here more this week than you're usually here in a month."

"The president of Columbia is making me do this job. I should be on the computer doing my research. Well, he's the boss, but he doesn't decide my pay raise."

Grant sent for me, and I gave him a rundown. He didn't look too well. Unusually deep circles under his eyes—down into his cheeks.

"I hate blackmailers. I didn't get much sleep last night. I'll have to taper off," I reported.

"Look, play this guy Henderson along. There's millions here."

"Millions and millions," I said, disgusted with him. "That's what my president said." I went to my small desk and ate my cheese Danish and savored my Dr. Pepper. I only wanted to teach and do research. This engagement was **not** typical of forensic accounting work.

Research. When would I ever learn to budget my time and factor in more research? It's no different than budgeting for a business. Failing to meet cash budget requirements can lead to dilemmas like one computer leasing company found, when the president discovered he could either meet the payroll or meet the bond payments—but there wasn't enough cash available to meet them both. Sort of like when I can work on forensic accounting cases like this one, or write and publish a technical research paper, but I can't do both at once.

That company president's fiduciary responsibility required that he meet the payroll first, which left no choice but to default on the bonds. The company had to declare bankruptcy. Fortunately, the president was able to find a larger company willing to buy out the creditors, and keep the company running. To someone responsible for operating a multimillion dollar, publicly traded company, that kind of stress can be damaging.

For a junior professor, the stress of failing to publish is heavy too. Trying to hit the top five journals is extremely difficult, which causes dysfunctional behavior, such as ignoring good teaching, grade inflation, and coursework deflation. But of course, being tenured, I mostly need to publish for raises, promotions, and favorable teaching and committee assignments. Publishing practitioner- type articles also helps me to bring new material into my classroom lectures, as does my forensic accounting work. All three really work well together. Good consulting engagements enhance the realism of my classroom teaching, and give me ideas for more relevant research, which helps get my name out in publications. When it all works right, there's a lot of synergy, and the students get a better education because of it. I also can help them network better in their job searches, through the contacts I make.

Tom called. "I'm calling from Masters's place on my cell phone," he said. "No lab scales. But there's a paint mixer. Can I keep it?"

"No," I said. "No pretty white powder, no waxy looking rocks? No forged masterpieces?"

"Nope. But there's a newspaper printed in Cyrillic. Couldn't make heads or tails out of it. Masters walked out with some woman, so I let myself into his apartment. Went through the service door. Piece of cake. Can't stay long 'cause I don't know when they'll be back."

"What did the woman look like?"

He described Nadja.

"She's Walker's model," I told Tom. "Probably models for Masters too. Better get out of there."

"Will do." He hung up.

I waited for Tom in the lobby, and we went for a late lunch. The rain had stopped, and the streets looked almost clean. We ordered Santa Fe chicken, and bacon-wrapped barbecue shrimp at a nearby restaurant.

I told Tom about Grant wanting me to play Henderson along. Tom shook his head in disgust. "That bum," he said. "He's got enough revenue. Why doesn't he just let this engagement go?"

"Maybe he wants to be in Henderson's social class."

"Right," Tom grinned. "I've read about Lloyd Henderson. He makes more money than some Hollywood directors."

"Myra hinted last night that there's something between her sister Sandra and Paul Manfred—they could be behind the blackmail threat."

"She's old enough to be his mother," Tom snorted.

"Don't tell me you've never heard of older women going out with younger men. Cougars. Sandra is in that big mansion, with no one to manipulate but Paul Manfred. Stranger things have happened."

"Sure, if pigs could fly. Would she set up her own father for blackmail?"

I shrugged. "She doesn't have any money of her own, according to Myra. So, she might want to make sure she gets some for herself, before the old man dies. Maybe kowtowing to him all the time has made her bitter."

"Look, let's say that's the game. Sandra and Paul against Henderson. Okay. But why fifty grand? That's chicken feed for a guy like Henderson. It doesn't make sense."

Tom had something there. "It does seem kind of odd. But if $50 thousand is only the first payoff with more to follow …"

"Sooner or later Henderson would be sure to catch on to whoever is squeezing him, especially if he has to keep making payments."

We kept on eating. The whole thing seemed out of whack. How did Teddy's death factor into the equation? Maybe they had nothing to do with each other.

It was getting chilly when we walked along the uncrowded sidewalk back to my second office, but not cold enough for coats again. We sat in my office and talked about how Teddy Noren's death might have fit into the puzzle.

"You really think he was murdered?" Tom asked.

"An auditor's intuition," I said.

"Then he probably knew about the blackmail plan," Tom concluded.

"Maybe. What about the art forgery business? He could have been ready to blow the whistle on whoever was—"

Tom shook his head. "Not if his girlfriend was involved, then he knew about it, or was part of it."

"We're just going around in circles." I felt like a dummy variable, which is used to represent the presence or absence of a condition in a regression model.

Hildy walked in and sat on the desk. "What are you gossips yacking about?" She has even, white teeth when she smiles.

I told her.

"I think I have the answer to the sixty-thousand-dollar question," Hildy said, almost taunting.

"Let's have it." I was interested. Hildy is one sharp cookie.

"Simple," she said. "To see if he'll bite."

I thought I knew what she meant. "Explain," I said.

"If he pays up, then the blackmailer will figure he really has Henderson hooked. He'll keep asking for more or ask for one big lump. On the other hand, if Henderson fights back, well, the blackmailer may just back off, figuring it isn't worth the effort."

"Henderson won't take the chance of not fighting back," I said. "He'll pay one and then fight like a tiger. He's not the kind to let anyone bleed him dry."

"You don't know," Hildy said. "Grandfathers can be protective of their grandchildren, even more than their own kids."

I had a feeling we weren't even close to what was really happening. We were dancing along the edges, skirting around the real issues, but not even close to the heart of what was going on.

Teddy's murder, forgery, artists, models, and blackmail. A lot of puzzle pieces, but put them all together and what did I get? Nothing. It was a jumbled mess. I just couldn't make it all fit—like many forensic accounting investigations. As most investigators know, sometimes you cannot catch a cold while trying to solve a problem.

I finally chased them out of my office and got on the phone. I called Marilyn Riley. She wasn't in. I tried Myra. "I was going to call you, Lenny" she said, "but —"

"Foolish pride?"

"Don't be silly. You might think I was chasing you."

"That's ridiculous. Have you heard anything from Marilyn?"

"Yes. This afternoon. She stopped over and borrowed some money. I think she should get out of that apartment. But she doesn't have the money."

"Did she say where she was going?"

"Shopping."

"I think Marilyn should move in and stay with you," I said. "Just for a few days."

"She'll crowd my kitchen."

"She's your daughter."

"I'll suggest it," Myra said coolly.

"How about dinner tonight, to try to solve this thing?"

"Okay, there's a nice place on Most Street," she said. "I feel like Chinese tonight."

"Seven okay? I'll pick you up."

"Okay." She hung up.

I did some more thinking but got nowhere. This mess was still a tangled disaster.

Too many fragments, and they didn't fit together. There had to be a link somewhere. How would I find it? This engagement was something like trying to solve standard cost variance problems. When you're trying to determine overhead variances there's different ways to slice and dice the data. There's one-way, two-way, and three-way analysis of overhead variances.

One-way, or a simple overhead variance calculation just compares the actual overhead cost with the overhead applied to production. It doesn't give much insight into why the difference occurred. Two-way analysis splits the variance into that caused by the variable overhead and that caused by the fixed overhead. The basic three-way overhead variance method splits the total overhead variance into a spending, an efficiency, and a volume variance. Basically, sometimes things just cost more. Other times, you may work efficiently, causing things like lighting, power, or supplies to decrease or increase in cost. Then, if production volume is higher or lower than the planned volume of production, you will have additional differences from expected overhead cost.

The three-way method usually separates variable cost overhead items from the fixed cost items. So, three-way analysis doubles, to make six-way analysis. But, two of the variances (the variable overhead volume variance and the fixed overhead efficiency variance), by construction, always equal zero. So, three-way analysis doubles to six-way, less two that are always zero, leaving four-ways—but we still call it three-way. I've seen some books that refer to four-way analysis of overhead variances. Guess it just keeps the students confused. On the other hand, a strong understanding can help the manager understand cause of the overhead variance.

I called Lloyd Henderson's office. Mr. Henderson was too busy to talk to anyone, I was told. I insisted they give my name to him. He finally got on the line. "Hear anything from our invisible friend?" I asked.

"No, Dr. Cramer." His voice was raspy. "If I had, I would have called you." There was a sharp click, and I was alone in the world, with all the rest of the disconnected underlings.

I had some unkind thoughts about my paying client, put on my coat, and told Hildy I would see her tomorrow. Maybe I'd put in a full day's work.

On the way home, somebody started to follow me, and stayed around for a solid hour. He was short, and his hair was the color of dark ginger. Young, stocky, in a gray suit. I let him follow me, so I could remember what he looked like. When I had his picture in my mind I played a few games with him, going around blocks, changing direction, going into stores. He had a partner, someone in a late model Nissan. Either my shadow wasn't too good, or he wanted me to know I was being watched. He stayed across the street, instead of behind me. Some fraud investigators learn to take a different route home every night.

When it was time to lose him, I did. He and his partner. I jotted down the plate number of the car, and that was all I needed.

Hildy was still in the office, so I called her on my cell phone and gave her the license plate number. Then I went to Myra's art gallery to check out her inventory. None of the paintings in the small shop or in the back inventory appeared to be obvious fakes. Then I went home. In the Jacuzzi I relaxed with a cold ginger ale. Having this whirlpool installed was one of the best decisions I ever made—it's the one thing about home I really enjoy. So, there was no connection between the art gallery and the fake paintings—at least not that I'd found.

When I met Myra, she was decked out with a teal green, embroidered silk dress, and a small beaded jacket. She had a jade pendant on a slender gold chain around her neck. She looked elegantly beautiful. A taxi took us to Chinatown. She reminded me of Burma.

I'd been in this restaurant before. Everything was good except the wonton soup. Someone boiled water and dragged a chicken feather through it. But the hard-boiled quail eggs wrapped in bacon—a real favorite.

"Did you talk to Marilyn?" I asked, trying my General Tso's chicken.

"She says she thinks you're wrong, and that she's not in any kind of danger, but she did agree to stay with me for the night. She stopped by to get a key."

She tasted my pungent chicken, and I tasted her shrimp in lobster sauce.

When we left it was dark and the street was crowded again. It took about five tries to get a taxi. Apparently, taxis were becoming scarce because of Uber.

# Seven

*So, the way to express the goal is this? Increase throughput while simultaneously reducing both inventory and operating expense.*

— Eliyahu M. Goldratt and Jeff Cox

An hour after I returned home I was asleep. Out cold. No nightmares this time.

The morning looked like it was going to be a cool day. But no drizzle. I ate breakfast and brushed my teeth. For some reason I recalled my usual classroom story that cost accounting should be effective and efficient. Brushing your teeth is the internal cost system. The resources that you use are toothpaste, water, floss, and labor. The bathroom is overhead. Effectiveness refers to whether you get your teeth clean. Efficiency refers to whether you waste water, floss, toothpaste, and lighting—lean accounting. Finally, can you do a better job of brushing your teeth?

A subway took me to the 116th Street and Broadway stop. When I came up out of the station, I was right in front of the massive gates to Columbia University.

The surrounding neighborhood is kind of dangerous, right next to Harlem. But on campus there's not much fear of street crime. The campus has trees and grass even in the heart of New York City. Stately pillared buildings.

In the center of the campus, I made my usual left turn and headed toward Uris Hall, where the Business School is located. The walk was peaceful, with trees on both sides of a clean brick walkway. Supposedly, there are some top-secret rooms in the building, and there are plans to move the business school to another building.

There was a memo on my desk. Call Henderson. I desperately needed to find a large block of uninterrupted time, to get ready for my upcoming expert witness testimony on another engagement. But when?

"Another letter came this morning," Henderson said. "I'm working at home today. When can I expect you?"

"Sometime this afternoon."

"Call before you leave. Paul will meet your train."

I called Grant's office. He had already heard from Henderson. "Henderson's blackmailer wants you to deliver the money personally."

"Why not Paul Manfred? I'm a lowly, underpaid professor."

"Maybe Henderson has something he wants to tell you," Grant said. "What's the difference? You've got to cater to your client. The customer is always right. We'll teach you how to be a real forensic accountant, Lenny. Maybe someday you can write a novel and get tenure."

"I already have tenure. Besides, novels don't count. Only technical research articles in esoteric refereed journals. Remember the novel *Love Story*? The author was denied tenure at Harvard."

Next, I called Hildy.

"I got the info on that license plate number yesterday," she reported. "It belongs to Sergei Relgado."

Who is Sergei Relgado?

"Sergei is an organized crime figure, with his fingers in a lot of different pies. Loan sharking, numbers, extortion, drugs. He's in the papers often, sometimes smiling with his arm around some tabloid star, and sometimes smiling standing next to a jockey or horse trainer. He's in his fifties, balding, with bulbous eyes. Good luck!"

When I got to Long Beach, it wasn't Paul Manfred who met me. It was Sandra Henderson. We'd only met once, during lunch at his mansion. She was behind the wheel of a silver Porsche 911 Turbo convertible, with a scarf around her head, dressed in black stretch pants and a madras shirt. She popped the lock on the passenger side door, and I got in.

"Where's Paul?" I asked.

"I told him I'd pick you up." She grinned at me and stepped on the gas. "I'm better company than Paul, anyway. He's dull."

"And you're just a bubbling cheerleader, is that it?"

"I'm happy when I feel like it. Today I feel happy. You missed lunch."

"I'll make up for it."

"How about dinner tonight?" she asked coyly.

"You're my client's daughter. How would that look?"

"Don't worry about him. My father can be stubborn, but I know how to handle him."

"I thought it was the other way around," I said.

She looked sharply at me.

A car was coming toward us, and she swerved hard, missed it by a few inches. She laughed, recklessly. "Do I have to drag you, kicking and screaming, to dinner?"

"Uh, no."

"Cora and I have been under my father's thumb for a long time. But I wiggle out occasionally. Cora wants to stay exactly the way she is. That's her problem," she added icily.

"Doesn't your father hold the check book?" I asked her.

"Yeah," she said seriously. "There's always that. Money. You can't have fun without money. But—" She stopped talking abruptly. Thinking she was talking too much? "Don't worry about me. Sandra is growing up. I'll find a way."

"With Paul?"

Her face turned kind of ugly. She glanced at me. "Who's been talking to you? That little vampire Myra?"

"No," I said. "Makes sense, doesn't it? Paul's a young guy, good-looking, and there's not much else to pick from in that big house of yours."

She faced the road and didn't say anything. That hit a nerve.... She and Paul. So, they were seeing each other. So, what? Why should she care about my knowing that? Unless there was something more to it.

She parked in front of the house, and we got out.

We walked up the flagstone front walk to the door, and she took me to her father's study. "I'll be out back," she said. "See me before you leave. Look, I'll drive you to the station, okay?"

"Sure." I opened the massive study door and went inside.

Mr. Henderson came straight to the point. "I've been sent instructions. Here they are. And here is $50,000, in 50s. You will deliver the money tonight. My first and last payment."

I read the letter. There was nothing in it but instructions for delivering the money. I put the letter and the money down. The money was in a brown expanding folder, taped down with the kind of packing tape you get in the post office. Mr. Henderson didn't look happy. I didn't feel happy.

"There's probably no fingerprints on it. Who else knows about this?" I asked.

"No one. Have you made any progress?"

"No," I said.

"You're not doing such a great job, are you? Even a blind pig finds an acorn sometimes. Well, no matter."

"Why do you want me to deliver the money?"

"Because I expect you will continue to assist me in keeping this whole thing quiet," he said. More of an assertion than an expectation.

"And while you're here, since you're a bean counter maybe you can help me with something else. I have an income statement from the CFO of one of my companies. He asserts that it's under the direct costing method. How does that differ from the normal income statement?"

"Absorption approach?"

"What?"

"The normal way is called the absorption approach. Direct costing also is known as variable costing. It is computed differently.

"How?"

"Absorption costing charges total materials, labor, variable overhead, and *fixed* overhead costs to inventory. Under Generally Accepted Accounting Principles (GAAP), it is used to value inventory and calculate cost of goods sold for *external* financial reports. A modified form of absorption costing is required by the IRS for tax purposes. It's used for product pricing decisions based on full costs. Cost of goods sold, of course."

I stopped for a tense moment, looked straight at Henderson and continued. "With variable costing, *fixed* overhead is not charged to the units of production — say memory chips. Instead fixed factory overhead is taken as an expense in the period in which it's incurred. It doesn't become part of the inventoried cost of the products."

"Then this fixed overhead is charged directly against sales, just like advertising and administration costs," he replied.

"That's right," I said.

"So why is he using this direct costing?"

"It's better for decision making. It doesn't allow period costs—like straight line depreciation on your plant and equipment—to be shifted across time periods as inventory levels go up or down."

"What do you mean, 'shifted?'"

"When fixed overhead costs are charged to a unit of product, they sit on the balance sheet in the asset account, Inventory. The fixed overhead doesn't get expensed right away. That's how absorption costing—the normal method—the GAAP method—works. If the inventory piles up, and the items aren't sold until the next period, that straight line depreciation gets shifted into the second time period. It gets expensed in the income statement as part of cost of goods sold *only* when the unit is sold—not in the period when the costs were incurred. That's the matching principle in accounting. Match revenues with expenses, just like debits match credits."

I again paused for a moment. "Anyone who's ever done taxes for a manufacturing company knows the importance of ending inventory in determining deductible cost of goods sold. The higher the ending inventory cost valuation, the lower the deductible cost of goods sold, and the higher the income tax. That's one reason the IRS requires absorption costing—to increase tax revenues over the short run. They even have a whole section called the Uniform Capitalization Rules, under Internal Revenue Code (IRC) Section 263A that specifically defines what costs *must* be capitalized into the asset account, Inventory. Should I continue?"

"Yes."

"Direct costing is theoretically superior because it doesn't allow a manager to shift fixed costs across time periods just by raising production to increase inventory levels. I saw an article once, called, 'How to Handle Manufacturers' and Processors' Inventories at Cost,' in *Tax Ideas*. It gives a solid illustration of how to apply the Section 263A rules. It's worth looking at. From a broader time perspective, as long as a company has some inventory, using absorption costing has put some of the fixed overhead into inventory, and therefore, the deductible expenses over time have been lower. Higher taxable income, and the IRS is happy."

I continued. "The Institute of Management Accountants has given seven examples for improved decision making. I'll send you a copy of their report. *Variable* or direct costing is an approach that corresponds more closely with the *current* cash outlays needed to manufacture products. Variable costing is more in sync with just-in-time inventory and lean accounting. No incentive for management to produce extra product." I sounded suspiciously like a professor in front of a classroom. This wasn't like Henderson. What was he after?

I decided to change the subject. "Do you have a copy of the serial numbers on these bills?"

"No. Whoever it is, I want him paid off and out of the picture. I don't want him caught so he can feed a lot of slander to the police and the news reporters."

I left his study and went outside to find Sandra. She was sitting on a bentwood rocker on the back porch, sipping something green out of a long stem crystal glass. She had changed into a cotton summer dress, the kind with a square neckline and short sleeves. Rebecca of Sunnybrook Farm. I sat down, and she asked if I wanted something to drink. I said no.

"What's Paul to you?" I asked.

"Someone to talk to. That's all."

I didn't believe her. "What's he to your father?"

"A bodyguard."

"That's all?"

"Call him a troubleshooter if you want."

"I want."

"I told my father not to expect me for dinner," she said. "Now you'll have to take me out."

I wanted to say something clever, but I couldn't think of anything. So, I grunted.

"I'm thinking about getting a buzzed hairdo like Dixie Chick Natalie Maines. What do you think?"

"Not wise," I responded. Who were the Dixie Chicks, I wondered? Who is Natalie Maines?

She finished her frothy drink and drove me to the train station. She called the house from the station and told someone to pick the car up. When the train arrived, we got on and sat down in an unusually quiet car.

"What do you think of my father?" she said.

"Another powerful businessman."

"He hates to spend a dime," she said. "And he has so much. There'll be more dimes when he gets his patent on that new design he has going. It's a faster, more powerful memory chip. Smaller than anything on the market. My father is a brilliant man, but he *can* be ruthless. His only love is his paintings. He's been collecting them for years."

Paintings? Teddy, Frank, and Bram were painters. Myra owned an art gallery, and Marilyn worked there. Now what was the connection?

"What kind of paintings?" I asked.

She shrugged her shoulders. "Good artists. The expensive ones. Picasso, Turner, Winslow—"

"You are kidding?"

"No. Why?"

"He must have a pretty elaborate security system," I observed.

She laughed. "Who was it? Edward G. Robinson said that a person doesn't collect paintings—paintings collect the person. They're all safe. We even have a special room. With all kinds of alarms, like for the McGuffey Art Center." Only my father can turn it off.

"I should hope so."

"Now let's talk about us."

We walked from Grand Central Station to an outside subway entrance. I hate the New York subways. Dirty, smelly, crime ridden. Not as nice as the ones in Russia, doubling as bomb shelters. Like rats underground. It seems like they find a dead body in the tunnels about once every day.

We went on to my apartment. I made her a cup of instant Cafe Francé, went into my bedroom, got ready for a shower. Sandra was busy listening to classical CDs, while I showered and shaved.

I went back into my bedroom after showering and put on clean clothes. I had left the money and the directions on my dresser at a certain angle, with a hair placed on top of them. Both had been moved, and the hair was gone. I knew Sandra must have picked them up. What would she gain from that? Was it curiosity? Or was the information for her—or for Paul? Why did she want to be with me while I had Henderson's package?

The phone rang before we left. It was Myra. I talked without mentioning her name. I told her I couldn't see her tonight, that I was working.

"Do I have a rival?" Sandra asked, as we went downstairs.

"We're just going to dinner," I told her. "Just dinner. Then you're going home."

"I don't like rejection," she said tightly.

"You'll have to grow on me," I said.

We had dinner at a place on the top floor of a bank. Then we went back to Grand Central for the train. I said goodbye, and I went to deliver the package.

It was dark, and the city was seething. From Grand Central, on 42nd Street, to Sixth Avenue there weren't too many people, but then, like a different world, they came out of the woodwork. The prostitutes, the pimps, addicts, dealers, the thrill seekers were everywhere. It was a crowded, bizarre menagerie in Times Square. The innocent, getting snared by temptation, mixing with those who lived under it every day.

Almost lost in the middle of this jungle I saw a small storefront, jammed between two sleazy joints. It had a small neon sign in the front window reading, "Jesus Saves." The young woman standing out front was handing out something. What was she doing here? It was as if her face was radiant. She had love for the urchins existing on this bottom rung of society. They never ceased to amaze me ... she had something I didn't. She walked up to me and handed me a blue leaflet. It was a small Gospel leaflet. I glanced at it, thanked her, and slipped it into my shirt pocket.

I kept walking toward Eighth Avenue, turned right, walked up past the honky tonks and dives. Outside a noisy lounge called Ned's I stopped to look at my watch. It was the right time.

"Hi, Bud."

I looked down at a dwarf. He had craggy features and a large belly, and he wore a seedy motorcycle jacket.

He looked up at me, happy like a kid with an ice cream cone. He looked like he was about 30, and his hair was oily black. A hunk of it fell over his pimply forehead.

"Got the package?" he said.

"What's the password?"

"What?"

"The password."

"What password?"

"Humor, my man."

I smiled and handed the folder to him.

It started to drizzle again. Crazy month, April. He stowed the money under his jacket, turned and whistled his way down the street. He bounced from side to side as he walked.

That was it. I'd delivered the money. No mishaps. I wasn't shot. Alleluia.

I went home. This assignment was surely not typical forensic accounting work.

Outside my door I fished for my keys. Then they appeared out of nowhere … the guy who'd been tailing me, and a man with bulbous eyes.

Sergei Relgado. He was unmistakable.

"Don't mind us," Sergei said. "Just go right on inside, and there won't be any trouble."

The other man had a hand in his charcoal jacket pocket. I didn't have a gun on me. Don't like having to carry a gun anyway. I do have a concealed hand gun permit. Well, a clear head would have to make the difference for now. They'd caught me blindsided. Even if I'd tried to go for a gun, I'd have been shot dead in my tracks.

So, I opened the door and went inside, followed by Sergei Relgado and his friend with yellow teeth.

I switched on the lights and sat down. The two took chairs. Relgado said, "You know who I am?"

"Sure," I said.

He was 55 if he was a day. I didn't like his oily voice.

"No, you don't."

Who was I to argue? "Okay. I don't."

Sergei grinned at his companion. "You see? A smart man. A very smart man."

The other red-faced man grunted.

Sergei reached inside his jacket and came out with the folder I'd given to the dwarf. These guys made good time. It'd been opened. He tossed it to me. I caught it. "Count it."

I counted. Fifty thousand dollars. It was all there. I tossed it back. "So?"

"So, nothing," Sergei said. "You delivered, and you did not take. I always expect the worst in people. How would you like to keep all of this money?"

I got to my feet and the companion pulled out his gun. "I need something to drink," I said.

"Put it away," Sergei grumbled. His friend put the black 9mm semiautomatic away, and I poured myself some iced tea. I sat down again.

"You did hear what I said, did you not?" Sergei said. He took a cheap smelling cigar from a breast pocket, clipped it with a cigar cutter, and stuck the thing in his mouth.

"Yeah. I heard you." I drank, as Sergei lit his cigar. "I prefer you not smoke in here. What's the catch?"

"The idea," Sergei said, "is for you wait until I give you orders, and then you do exactly what I tell you."

"I'm not my own boss."

He grinned at me. "I am knowing this. You are also knowing who I am now, so you can call me Sergei. But nobody is to know I was here talking with you—that is our little secret. Now Hossein here, is someone I can trust. If I tell Hossein to cut your throat, he will do this dirty deed for me. If I tell him to plant you in the woods so nobody will find you again, he will do this, also. I would hate to deprive your students of your insightful lectures, Dr. Cramer. Do we have an understanding?"

I told him I got it. Loud and clear.

"I want you to be available for something," Sergei said. "Fifty thousand dollars is a lot of money. Do you not think?"

"Why me?"

"Because you are now in the middle. You have been, as you say, suckered, Dr. Cramer. You can have this money right now. You see? I trust you. Do I not, Hossein? Do you want these fifty thousand dollars now? Or do you not?" He demanded.

"I have a client. I have a boss."

"Do not be stupid," he barked. "Are you some kind of actor?" His face got dark. "I come to you in good faith. I offer you fifty thousand dollars. And you give to me some kind of act. I am not liking this. Do you understand?" He demanded. "Are you in, or are you out?" He glowered menacingly.

"You haven't told me what this deal is all about." Sure, I was stalling. I needed information.

Relgado sighed. "You will know what you need when it is time."

"I'll have to think about it."

Hossein pulled his gun out again. "Let me 'explain' it to him. I will help him to make up his mind."

I was beginning to dislike Hossein. I looked at Sergei. "It would be nice if I knew what I was getting into."

Sergei stood up. Hossein stood up.

"Put the gun away," Sergei said, brushing Hossein aside with his hand. Hossein did what he was told. But he didn't look happy about it. His little power trip was being spoiled.

Bulbous eyes stared at my face. "Twenty-four hours. That is all I give to you. You will give me an answer by then." He left, followed by helpful Hossein.

I locked the door and made myself another cold drink. Wasn't feeling too well. I didn't like being threatened, but then, who did?

My daughter Rebecca called, and we talked for a few minutes. I'm proud of Rebecca, and I miss her. She was doing well in college.

I looked out the window and didn't see anyone hanging around. It was still drizzling. I put my .45 under the bed and went to bed. Before going to sleep, I picked up the little Gospel leaflet I'd gotten from the girl in Times Square. I looked it over and read it. It made sense. I switched off the light and drifted into a surprisingly restful sleep for a change.

# Eight

*Under a job order cost system, the three basic elements of cost—direct materials, direct labor, and factory overhead—are accumulated according to assigned job numbers. The unit cost for each job is obtained by dividing the total units for the job into the job's total cost. A cost sheet is used to summarize the applicable job costs.*

—R.S. Polimeni, F.J. Fabozzi, and A.H. Adelberg

I got to the accounting office early, and when Tom came in I had him join me. He listened as I told him about my delivering the money to the dwarf, and the later visit by Sergei and Hossein.

"Twenty-four hours, huh?"

"That's it," I said. "Twenty-four hours to make up my mind for Mr. Bulbous eyes."

Tom was amused. "What are you going to do?"

"Start packing."

"I'd better stick to you like white on rice."

"Well, I'd appreciate that. I'd also appreciate a whole army. That Hossein fellow looks trigger happy."

"But where does Relgado fit into this whole mess?"

I shrugged my shoulders. "Don't ask me. But that fifty grand was a test for sure. Somebody's after a bigger jackpot."

"Like what?"

"I don't know. Maybe more money. A ton of money."

"So, with Henderson forking over the fifty grand, Relgado gets the idea he's a pushover?"

"That's the best theory we've got so far," I said. "Unless Sergei is trying to muscle in on somebody's racket somewhere."

Hildy walked into the office.

We told Hildy everything, on the condition it wasn't to be repeated to John Grant. Grant liked things simple. He wouldn't like the idea that somebody thought one of his partners could be bought for $50 thousand dollars—even under duress.

I'd tell Grant what I thought he needed to know, and no more.

Later, Tom and I went down for lunch. He asked me why I didn't take the money.

I pretended shock. "I'm an honest guy. And I'm a CPA, among other things."

"Fifty thousand bucks is 50 thousand bucks," Tom said flatly. "Why don't you take the money and run." He munched on bread and meat. "What's Relgado going to do, go to the police?"

I drank some of my Coke. "He could send Mr. Hossein after me."

Tom dismissed Hossein with a wave of his hand. "A punk. Take that gun out of his hand and what have you got? A spineless thug."

"I've got no intention of testing that hypothesis. Thug or no thug."

"No fifty thousand bucks?"

"No fifty thousand bucks," I echoed.

"Then I suggest you take one of the .45s from the office. We have an excellent selection, and they're all in top condition."

"I've got one. But I'm not much of a shot. Out at the range, what I lack in accuracy I make up for by being inconsistent."

"I'd better stick with you then," Tom said. "By the way, I looked over the books at Myra's gallery. Everything seems okay to me. I didn't spot any signs of embezzlement. No revenues unsupported by purchase invoices or consignment slips—unless, of course, what I found were fakes. It's a small business. They could be selling anything. But guess who loaned the gallery money? Your buddy Sergei Relgado—$120,000."

"Wow! Has any of the loan been paid back?"

"Yep. The original loan was for $520,000. Four hundred thousand has been paid back. What do you think of that?"

"Was there evidence of any cash on hand at the time the loan was made?"

"That's a good question," Tom said. "I couldn't find any. I'll have to check a little more though. There's a huge amount for paintings on consignment. Try this one on. Relgado fronts the gallery cocaine, instead of cash. The gallery sets up a loan payable. Maybe the offsetting debit is to Paintings Inventory or something—I need to check more. In any event, the gallery then sells the crack, takes a cut, and funnels the rest of the money back to Relgado under the guise of loan repayments. A cute way to launder drug money," Tom smiled cynically.

"When you go back, try to find if fake paintings are being sold to just a few customers—at inflated prices. Counting inventory held on consignment as part of a firm's own inventory will overstate the assets. That could offset the loan as you suspect. With artwork, it doesn't have to be a lot of inventory to come up to those amounts. As you said, check it out some more."

"Good idea," Tom responded. "Oh, here's a list of some of the art work they sold over the past year. Maybe you can tell if they're booked at fair market values."

I put the list into my briefcase, and snapped it closed. I thought about my predicament. I'm a CMA—Certified Management Accountant—maybe in this situation it stood for Certified Maniac Association. The CMA is a certificate from the Institute of Management Accountants (IMA). They have 100,000 members, but some are not certified. There are about 30,000 CMAs in the U.S. The IMA has an important code of professional ethics.

I also have my CPA license—Certified Public Accountant—as well as the CRFAC-Certified Forensic Accountant. The American Institute of CPAs give the CPA exam. They have more than 664,000 members—many of them practice in public accounting. Whereas, the IMA is made up of accountants who work for companies. With the public accounting market growing less than management accounting, both organizations are vying to dominate the field of management accounting.

The material tested on the CMA exam has a broader scope than the CPA exam. The CMA exam covers economics and finance, information systems, quantitative methods, internal and external reporting—with heavy emphasis on cost and managerial accounting—and organizational behavior and ethics.

The CMA exam is not 60 percent multi-choice like the CPA exam. The CMA exam has a heavy emphasis on essays, and analytical problem solving. The CMA has two parts with each test containing 100 multiple choice questions and two essays. I can still remember studying from Irv Gleim's *CMA Examination Review* manual.

The difference between a CPA and a CMA is like the umpire and pitcher in a baseball game. A CPA auditor is like the umpire. He or she makes sure the appropriate external reporting rules are followed. On the other hand, the CMA is like a pitcher trying to win the game—executing the best strategy and beating the competition.

About 70 percent of accounting graduates take entry-level jobs in business, government, and education. Less than 30 percent go straight into public accounting, and 75 percent of them move to industry in less than 10 years. So, 90 percent of accountants end up working in managerial accounting roles eventually. You'd think that would make the CMA more popular.

Tom went to get a root beer. "Listen," he said, sitting down and giving me a mug filled with amber colored sugar water. "What does Sergei have to do with that dead artist of yours? What's his name? Teddy Noren?"

"I don't know. I can't see Relgado shooting somebody and then painting a picture."

"And Sergei wouldn't cook up a suicide cover. He'd just have the guy blown away and disappear without a shred of evidence."

I drank the cold root beer. It felt soothing going down my throat. "We'll figure it out somehow."

"Are you going to tell Henderson that Relgado has the fifty grand?"

"I don't think so. I was told to deliver it, and that's exactly what I did."

"What now?"

"You stick around for now. I'm going to see Myra Riley."

"When do I get to stick with you?"

"My 24 hours isn't up yet."

"How old is this Myra, anyway?"

"Forty-something."

"Too old for me. But when I get to be your age...."

\* \* \*

"She can't just stay locked up here forever," Myra said. "She had a modeling job this morning. Should be home soon."

"Do you know someone named Sergei Relgado?" I watched her face, and her hands for clues of stress. But her eyes distracted me. Anyway, verbal and nonverbal indicators are often unreliable.

She shook her head. "No."

"Marilyn never mentioned him to you?"

"No. Never heard of him. Why?"

"Well, according to the books at your art gallery, Sergei Relgado loaned your gallery $520,000, and you still owe him $120,000."

"What?" she reached over and grabbed my hand. "I don't know anything about it. Maybe Marilyn borrowed the money."

"He's not exactly your friendly Wall Street banker."

She withdrew her hand. She was getting tense. She was almost hyperventilating. "That's between our creditors and Marilyn. We sometimes have a cash flow situation at the gallery. Marilyn takes care of it, Mr. Cramer." Her voice was a bit scornful but laced with a dignified embarrassment.

"Could Marilyn be selling fake paintings through your gallery? How about laundering drug money?"

"Absolutely not!"

Just then Marilyn walked in, loaded down with groceries. She didn't seem thrilled to see me. Myra helped her put things away in the kitchen. Then we sat and had iced tea.

I looked at them. Mother and daughter. There was a resemblance all right. Marilyn was younger and built for speed, but a little scorched around the edges. But when it came to perseverance, my money was on Myra. I had a feeling Marilyn would crash and burn within a few years.

"Have you seen Bram or Frank?" I asked her.

"I saw Bram yesterday. He was nice to me. I think you're paranoid."

"Maybe I am."

"I wish you'd listen to Mr. Cramer," Myra said.

"He's a doctor, Mom, and get off my case. You're all chasing shadows. Teddy killed himself, period. It's hard enough to deal with. Just let me get over it."

"Well that would simplify everything," I said. "Let's just hope you're right." I lifted my glass to my mouth. "Do you know a Sergei Relgado?"

Her face was wooden. Her eyes were on me, but I couldn't see any stress behavior around them.

Her lips moved slightly. "No."

Myra wanted to change the subject. "It's too early for dinner." She took hold of my hand. "You are eating with us, aren't you?"

"Sure. Why not."

A little later we had dinner. Myra was a decent cook. When we finished, Marilyn announced she had a date. "I'll leave you two here alone."

Myra wanted me to stay longer, but I said no. I promised maybe we'd see a movie and have dinner tomorrow night. Before I left the apartment building I called the office on my cell phone. Tom was there.

"I think you forgot about me."

"Who, me?" I feigned.

"I was interviewing some suspects. You know Fiddlers' Green on 38th Street?"

"So."

"Meet me there. We've got some things we need to talk about."

"Sure," I said to Tom.

"Okay. See you there." He hung up.

When I got to Fiddler's, Tom was already there. We sat in a booth. The table had a bowl of pretzels. "You'd better stay at my place tonight," Tom suggested.

"No good," I said. "Hiding in a cave is not going to help. If I can get Relgado to talk—"

"He'll talk with a 9mm."

"He said I was suckered. I want to know what he meant by that."

"Why don't you go to his place and ask?"

"His place?"

"While you were playing Romeo, I was working," Tom announced scoldingly. "Nothing like the telephone to call in a few IOUs on the street. Sergei owns a club called the Antalya Room, on 53rd Street. He's also got a new flame named Jeannette."

"How did you get all that?"

"Pays to have friends," Tom said. "I know a few folks who've got their ears wired."

\* \* \*

The Antalya Room had a tuxedoed door attendant who looked more like a gorilla in black-tie. He nodded at us and opened the door as we entered. The first thing that hit you was a smell of limes, liquor, and sizzling lamb shish kabob. Middle Eastern cuisine. But like a cheap nightclub out of a dollar novel.

The music pounded us as we walked into the main club room. A live band was playing on a stage at the far end. The singer was a female—slim, serpentine. One of the guitars looked like it was made from polished black onyx. It had a flowing red scarf tied to the end of the neck. What a way to make a living. There was a service bar, tables, and upholstered booths. Three servers scurried around with trays. There was Sergei, at a center table, with two Turkish-looking men and a woman. The woman had black hair, high cheek bones, and was wearing a silver dress like a tabloid star.

As we walked to a booth Relgado saw me, but his face was impassive. The woman glanced at me, then turned away. She put a hand on Sergei's arm and said something. She looked 40 but was probably just over it. Her makeup made the corners of her eyes look pointed.

A waiter came to our booth, I ordered my usual virgin Piña Colada, and she walked away.

"So, how do you like Sergei's new flame?" Tom asked.

"I like her fine. That black hair's cute too. Too bad it's a wig. Take it off and you'll find a blonde. A honey blonde named Sandra Henderson."

Tom didn't turn his head to look at Sandra. He was too experienced for that. "What?!"

"You've got me," I said, baffled.

No sooner had the waitress brought us our drinks, then Sergei was standing in front of our booth. He put a meaty hand on the red lacquered table. He ignored Tom, spoke straight to me. "You have a big mouth, professor." Oblique light made his face more menacing than it was, shadowing his heavy eyebrows, the full lips of his beefy face. "I do not think I can trust you anymore." The people at his table were looking at us. Except for Sandra-Jeannette. She was looking down at her table, at the drink in her hand, at the band, anywhere but in our direction.

"What are you talking about?"

"Do not give me any more of your acts, Dr. Cramer."

Tom's forearm was under the table. "If you think you can't trust me," I said, "then I'll just have to pass on your generous offer."

He looked smugly at Tom for the first time. "This man is not so smart as he thinks." He saw Tom's wooden face. Maybe he realized Tom had a gun on him. He straightened up, his lips twisting into a sinister grin. "Enjoy yourselves here gentlemen. Spend your money. We will discuss this business later."

"One question, Sergei," I said. "You said I was suckered into this situation. What were you talking about?"

"You say, suckered?" He looked like he was enjoying this game. "I am afraid you must be mistaken. Enjoy yourself. Spend your money." He walked confidently back to his table.

Tom's right hand came back into sight.

"You had a gun on him?"

"It kinda just fell into my hand," Tom said. The waitress came and took away our glasses.

"This dump is boring," Tom complained.

"Just watch Relgado's table."

Sergei's girlfriend whispered something close to his ear and got up from the table. She slid past waitresses and customers who were looking for tables and booths. I slipped out from our booth and followed her. She went into the restroom. I waited.

Two women with men old enough to be their fathers walked past. I waited.

When Sandra came out I confronted her. "I think we'd better talk."

"I am afraid I do not know you."

"Look, Sandra——"

"My name is Jeannette."

"Okay. Jeannette."

She looked worried. "Not now." She drew close to me. "Not now," she spoke softly into my ear.

"When?"

"Tomorrow … afternoon. I'll call your office."

"You'd *better*."

She gave my arm a squeeze with her dark blue painted fake fingernails and slipped past me. The pieces of this puzzle were not fitting together any better.

I went back to our booth. Tom and the waitress were acting like they were engrossed in a deep conversation. She smiled at me. Her hair was auburn, and her face was powdered with freckles. Kind of cute.

I sat down. "Sandra, or Jeannette will call the office tomorrow. Don't ask me what she's up to. She looked a little scared to see me here."

"That's a surprise," Tom said, mocking.

"Scared I'll blow her plans, whatever she's up to. She'll *have* to talk to me."

"Ahh, she'll probably just blow you off."

"Maybe."

Relgado and his entourage left their table and walked into a back room. "Too bad we couldn't get all that money from him," Tom said.

"You wanting to try?"

"No, thanks. I'm not that crazy. Just thinking of what I could do with it."

The night air was getting cool by the time we left the Antalya Room. The door attendant signaled to a cab for us. Tom gave him a tip.

"Well, we put in a full day today," I remarked.

Tom gave the driver my address.

"Didn't get a thing out of Relgado," I said irritated. "Except finding out that Sandra wears a black wig and looks like she's got a secret life on the arm of a Black Sea mobster. We really didn't get much, did we?"

# Nine

*Accounting for management is not management, and it should not be thought of as such. But accounting can be made to serve managerial purposes ... and it can help management to do a better job than could be done without it.*

—William J. Vatter

The next morning, in my accounting office, I noticed a small spider's web on the ceiling, in a dusty corner. My first impulse was to get a broom and sweep it away. That's what people usually do. But I didn't. I studied the web, but I didn't see the spider. Where was he hiding? Or she? How much did I know about spiders anyway?

If I got rid of that web, the spider would just come back and spin another one. No, leave it for now. Wait for the spider to come out. Maybe I can get the spider and the web all at one time. He or she probably had a lease anyway— just no rent control.

I missed seeing my daughter. I'd be glad when she came home for summer vacation—that is, if she didn't go to summer school.

I tried to concentrate on the Henderson mess, but it just gave me a splitting headache. It was too jumbled. Too many pieces to the puzzle. Too many questions and no answers. There had to be a solution somewhere.

Why was Teddy Noren killed? Why leave an oil painting in his apartment? Someone who mostly used acrylics? Who did the painting? Walker? Masters? Someone else I hadn't met yet? What was the connection to the art gallery? The loan from Relgado? Were faked paintings also being sold to launder drug money?

Who was blackmailing Henderson? I couldn't see Relgado in that role, even if he did have the $50,000. Henderson was a tough guy, but where did he fit into the money puzzle?

And I couldn't forget Sandra's "Jeannette" routine. Sandra and Paul Manfred. Sandra and Sergei Relgado. Sandra in a black wig. Did Sergei know his little Miss Jeannette was Sandra Henderson, heir to the mighty Lloyd Henderson?

What was Sandra's web?

I supposed when I had the answers, it would all be clear as primary earnings per share under Topic 260 of the FASB Codification — if I ever got the answers.

Then I spotted him. From where I sat he was just a dot, but I saw him all right, crawling up one of the threads.

All those threads to build a web. It made me think of a job order cost system. You identify each job physically and segregate all the costs of the job. Direct materials, direct labor, just like on the strands of a web, they're carried to each particular job number. Maybe the spider was factory overhead being applied to the job based upon a predetermined factory overhead application rate. No, I'm losing my mind. My brain is fried right now. Too much thinking, too many questions, very little answers.

All my ponderings of webbier allegory dissolved with the annoying jangle of the telephone. It was my friend Henderson.

"I haven't heard from you."

"I delivered it. That's all I can say for now."

"Did you get a look at them."

"Would you believe it? He was a fat dwarf. Somebody's go-between."

"I'm in the city, in my office, in case you have need to call me."

"You heard from anyone?"

"No. I would tell you if I had." He hung up.

An hour later sweetheart Sandra called. "Where can we meet?"

"You tell me."

"Have you told my father …"

"No," I replied.

"Let's have lunch somewhere. I'm in town. How about the deli on 42nd Street?"

"In an hour?" I said.

"Okay."

"Don't wear your wig," I chided.

Tom was in our accounting office. I told him where I would meet Sandra, and he should follow her when we left.

Sandra was at a corner table, waiting for me. We took trays and went down the cafeteria type line to get what we wanted and went back to the Formica and aluminum table. She had a huge carnelian ring on her right hand the size of a marble.

We talked as we ate.

"You've got to understand what I've been through all these years ... catering to my father," she said. "I was suffocating. I had to get out once in a while. But I couldn't afford to alienate my father. I went out with Paul a few times for dinner and some dancing. Paul couldn't always get away. Then I started getting out on my own. I met Sergei. He's a lot older than me, but I found being with him is so much more thrilling than my sheltered life in that house. He likes me and likes showing me off. And I like that — I like it a lot."

She saw I didn't believe her, so she shrugged and finished her lunch. "You've got me in an awkward position. What can I say? What can I do to keep you quiet?"

"Try telling me the truth."

"But I am," she protested.

"What are you and Sergei planning for your father?"

"Nothing."

"Sergei has $50,000 of your father's money. Blackmail money. You know what it's about. Stop playing games with me."

"I don't, Lenny. Really, I don't."

"Why the wig?"

"A whim. I didn't want people to recognize me"

"Does Sergei know who you really are?"

"No. How could he?"

"Does Paul Manfred know you're seeing Sergei?"

"No."

"Your father doesn't suspect where you're going?"

"I'm extremely ... careful."

"Some coincidence. You meet Sergei, go out with him, and he puts the bite on your father. But he doesn't know who you are. And you expect me to buy all this?"

"Fifty thousand dollars is nothing to Sergei."

That's what I thought too. I was sure he had bigger criminal operations than what even Tom's network knew about. But what was the answer? Was there any truth in what she was telling me? If I pressed her, she might cook up another lie to cover the first ones. Would Sandra even know the truth if she fell over it? To some people, truth is whatever is expedient to say now. Whatever they think will make them look good. "I think I'll get another cup of coffee."

"Go ahead. Get me another one too, would you?"

She said I had her in an awkward position, but she didn't seem worried about it today. Was it all just a stall? Was Relgado using her, or were she and Paul manipulating Relgado? Sergei wasn't the kind of person to be used or played for a fool.

I came back with the coffee and sat down.

"What are you going to do?" she said as she spooned sugar into her cup.

"I don't know yet."

"I don't have money to pay you anything." Her topaz eyes glowed with something akin to hate. Then she laughed shrilly. She didn't finish her coffee. She stood up. She put her palms on the table and leaned over toward me, eyes taunting mine. "Every man has his price, Lenny. Make up your mind what you want." She stalked out of the deli.

People were eating food and gulping down coffee. No one was wearing shorts. They would when it was the middle of May. It seemed like the summers were getting longer. Global warming is fine with me. I was getting hungry again, for a ham and cheese sandwich.

Outside, I used my cell phone and got the office. "Any messages?" I asked Hildy.

"Marilyn Riley called twice. Wants to see you. That's about it."

I thanked her and took a Metro bus downtown. I went to Marilyn's apartment in SoHo.

She was in shorts and a tee-shirt. "Too early for shorts," I said.

"Sit down. Want a drink?"

I sat down. I didn't want a drink. "You wanted to see me?"

Her hair was loose around her shoulders. "I had a talk with Bram today. I told him I don't want to sell for him anymore. He said I had no choice. If I tried to quit he would tell my grandfather."

"Did he kill Teddy?"

"Nobody killed Teddy."

"What about that oil painting?"

She said she didn't know.

"Why would Teddy want to kill himself?"

"I don't know. I thought about it a lot. I don't have any answer."

"Why is money disappearing from your mother's art gallery?"

"Art is down. We're not selling much. Customers are hard to find these days."

"Tell me about the loan from Sergei Relgado."

She rose to her feet and started pacing. "Look I can't cope with this anymore." She put the back of her hand to her forehead for a moment. "I'm not a strong person. I thought I could handle this. This just isn't happening to me. Look, you must do something. I can't let Bram go to my grandfather."

Was this some kind of an act? I thought of Paul Manfred. "I don't think Bram will get within two blocks of your grandfather."

"If, if you're thinking about Paul, … forget it. Paul does whatever Sandra tells him," she stuttered.

"What a family," I thought.

"All right … I'm, I'm all right," she said hastily, taking short, quick breaths. She sat down again, her face in her hands. Her body was noticeably shaking.

"Are you that afraid of Bram?"

She looked at me, a forced grin was pasted on. "I'm more afraid of my grandfather than Bram. He can be merciless."

"According to your mother, he likes you."

"As much as he can like anyone," she snapped. "Will you see Bram, talk to him or something?"

"What you want me to do is scare him off?" I was really getting tired of her, tired of this whole crazy family. What was I accomplishing? Too many loose threads. Too many forks in the road. Too many unexplained variances from standard costs. I thought about how a variance is the difference between *actual* results and *planned* results in a business organization. Management uses variance analysis to control costs. How many of these plans were panning out differently from Marilyn's intentions?

The trouble with cost accounting is variance analysis anyway, I thought cynically. When comparing actual direct labor hours in a plant with standard direct labor hours, minimizing idle time does not necessarily maximize profit. It's better to have idle time than to have too much inventory. Nobody in this family had been idle. They were building up a miserable inventory. Many systems do not penalize managers for maintaining too much inventory, they actually reward it. Many systems also penalize managers for idle time. So, most managers would rather increase inventory to reduce idle time.

Like I told Henderson, under the full (or absorption) costing system that most companies use, increasing last quarter production will increase ending inventory levels. That reduces cost of goods sold for the period, relative to a variable costing system—and thus increases the current year's reported profits. That happens until the effect reverses itself in another period. I thought of the example I give my students—where variable costs of production are $1.50 a unit, and fixed costs of production are $50,000, variable selling expenses are $.30 a unit, and fixed administrative costs are $20,000. When the company produces 100,000 units, the full costing system cost of producing one unit is $1.50 variable + ($50,000 / 100,000 units) = $2.00 per unit. Under a variable costing system that cost is simply the $1.50 variable production cost. Assume a First-In-First-Out (FIFO) physical flow of inventory, and you get

**Full Costing:**

| | | |
|---|---|---|
| Sales | (100,000 units x $3.00) | $300,000 |
| Beginning inventory | (10,000 units x $2.00) | $ 20,000 |
| Add: Cost of production | (100,000 units x $2.00) | 200,000 |
| Less: Ending inventory | (10,000 units x $2.00) | (20,000) |
| Cost of goods sold | (100,000 units) | (200,000) |
| Gross Profit | | $100,000 |
| Less: Operating costs: | | |
| Selling expenses | (100,000 x $0.30) | ( 30,000) |
| Administrative costs | | (20,000) |
| Net income | | $ 50,000 |

But for variable costing you get:

**Variable Costing:**

| | | |
|---|---|---|
| Sales | (100,000 units x $3.00) | $300,000 |

| Beginning inventory | (10,000 units x $1.50) | $15,000 |
| Add: Cost of production | (100,000 units x $1.50) | 150,000 |
| Less: Ending inventory | (10,000 units x $1.50) | ( 15,000) |
| Cost of goods sold | (100,000 units) | (150,000) |
| Variable selling expenses | (100,000 x $0.30) | ( 30,000) |
| Contribution margin | | $120,000 |
| Fixed production costs | | ( 50,000) |
| Fixed administrative costs | | ( 20,000) |
| Net income | | $ 50,000 |

If managers raise production to reduce idle time of production workers, under a full costing system the new cost per unit become $1.50 + ($50,000/125,000 units) = $1.90 per unit, and I show them what happens to cost of goods sold, and to profits as the ending inventory increases by 15,000 units:

**Full Costing:**

| Sales | (100,000 units x $3.00) | $300,000 |
| Beginning inventory | (10,000 units x $2.00) | $ 20,000 |
| Add: Cost of production | (125,000 units x $1.90) | 237,500 |
| Less: Ending inventory | (35,000 units x $1.90) | (66,500) |
| Cost of goods sold | | (191,000) |
| Gross profit | | $109,000 |
| Less: Variable selling expenses (100,000 x $30) | | (30,000) |
| Less: Fixed administrative costs | | (20,000) |
| Net income | | $ 59,000 |

**Variable Costing**

| Sales | (100,000 units x $3.00) | $300,000 |
| Beginning inventory | (10,000 units x $1.50) | $ 15,000 |
| Add: Variable cost of prod | (125,000 units x $1.50) | 187,500 |
| Less: Ending inventory | (35,000 units x $1.50) | ( 52,500) |
| Variable cost of goods sold | | (150,000) |
| Variable selling expenses | (100,000 x $30) | ( 30,000) |
| Contribution margin | | $120,000 |
| Fixed production costs | | ( 50,000) |

| | |
|---|---|
| Fixed administrative costs | ( 20,000) |
| Net income | $ 50,000 |

So, raising inventory, without a corresponding increase in sales, increases current year reported profits under full costing. Neat trick. Pull that one off, then move on to a new job. You leave on a high, then everything falls to pieces after you're gone. The IRS requires a modified full costing, of course.

The $9,000 difference in profit between the full and variable costing systems can be reconciled if you try. The 10,000 unit beginning inventory was produced in the previous period. But under a FIFO—First In First Out—physical flow assumption, it was sold in the current period. So, the beginning inventory carries $0.50 a unit, or a total of $5,000 of last period's fixed production costs into the current period's cost of goods sold.

On the other hand, the 35,000 unit ending inventory was produced in the current time period. It's still not sold, and will carry $0.40 a unit, or $14,000 of current period fixed production costs on the balance sheet as an asset, until it's sold in the next time period. At that time, it becomes a part of cost of goods sold for that year. So, $5,000 of last year's fixed costs are carried into this year's cost of goods sold, while $14,000 of this year's fixed costs are deferred on the balance sheet and carried into next year's cost of goods sold. The difference is a net reduction in current year cost of goods sold of $9,000. That's what increased the current year profit by $9,000. I usually show it this way:

| | | |
|---|---|---|
| Fixed costs in beginning inventory | (10,000 units x $0.50) | $5,000 |
| Fixed costs in ending inventory | (35,000 units x $0.40) | (14,000) |
| Net reduction in cost of goods sold | | ($9,000) |

When interpreting variances, just because a variance looks unfavorable, does not mean somebody did something wrong. On the other hand, just because a variance is favorable, doesn't mean somebody did something right. The standards used could be bad. Just think about the production manager faced with having to use up a load of poor quality raw materials. No matter how efficient a job he does getting quality product out of that material, his usage variance will look lousy next to the budget.

At the same time, the purchasing agent who bought the crummy materials will be gloating over his *coup* in getting such a great buy—look at his favorable materials price variance. And he did a great job getting in the shipment under rush order conditions.

And for what? Because the sales manager brought in a last minute, unbudgeted order, and no one anticipated the demand. And the sales manager was proud of his favorable sales quantity variance. After all, the order was brought in at the last minute by the company's biggest customer. They said if he couldn't meet their order, they'd take it across the street to our competitors. Thought he'd done a good job to snag the order. Earned a healthy commission on the sale too. If I had a dog, I think I'd name it Fifo.

"Will you see him?"

She jarred my thoughts from my theoretic digression. "What good will that do? Just more idle time," I muttered.

"What? It might help," she said hurriedly. "Bram's no tough guy. You're getting paid to help us, aren't you?"

Even if I did try to scare Bram Walker off, would that change anything for Marilyn? She'd get hooked on other creeps in place of Bram Walker and Frank Masters. If this little fly managed to escape from the web, she'd fly right into another one. I'd met people like Marilyn before. The woods were full of them. Classic co-dependent. Thought they were tough cookies, but they care what other people think of them too much. They'll pay almost any price to avoid rejection.

I stood up. "Okay. I'll talk to Bram. But I can't promise anything. I can't exactly slug him and heave him onto a train headed west."

"I know," she said.

"Now, tell me about the loan by Sergei to your mother's art gallery."

She looked surprised. "What's there to tell. We needed the money. I borrowed it from Sergei. There's no law against borrowing money."

"What interest rate are you paying?" I asked steadily.

"I don't remember. I'd have to look it up."

"Did your mother know about the loan?"

"Yeah. She knows everything about the gallery."

* * *

I saw Nadja hurrying out of her apartment building. She didn't see me. She was in light blue pants and a matching shirt, with a string of white pearls around her neck. The pearls danced as she dashed across the street and jumped into a waiting car. The driver was a young woman. The car raced off.

It was afternoon, and the sun was warm. I wished I was back in the library working on a managerial accounting literature review, but instead I went in to see Bram Walker.

He wasn't seeing anyone. Not today. Not tomorrow. His door was open, and I walked into his apartment. He greeted me with a dead silence.

The gun was on the carpet near his body, and there was a pool of blood. His eyes were stark open, looking out at eternity. I would bet anything that his fingerprints were on that gun. Looked like another suicide. Another waste. I went through the place. No scales, no wax, and no art forgeries this time. Oil paintings on canvases, an easel, brushes, and tubes of paint. That was about it. There was a thin, oval palette on the floor. Near it was a palette knife with red paint on the blade. It was time for me to beat it. So much for warning Bram off for Marilyn.

Outside, in the afternoon sun, I walked slowly. People always remember someone running or walking too fast. Somebody would remember Nadja. I walked along, thinking. Teddy Noren dead. Bram Walker dead. Two artists. Two small time drug dealers. Had some serial killer decided to rid the world of artists? Was Frank Masters still alive? I'd pay Masters a visit. What would be my reason for visiting Frank? I couldn't very well say, "Just wanted to make sure you were still alive." I'd think of something by the time I got there.

The law said I should report a dead body. Shouldn't leave the scene of a crime. Well, somebody else would have to have that pleasure today. I didn't want a swarm of police around my neck right now. Fox News and CNN would say, "Columbia Accounting Professor Finds Dead Artist."

Frank Masters was at home. Surprisingly he was in a jovial mood. "Come in," he said. "Sit down. Where's the little maid Marilyn?"

I sat down. "I just left her on a merry-go-round, licking an ice cream cone."

"A beautiful image, but a child's emotions, I'm afraid."

"The kind you can manipulate," I said.

"I suppose some people would think like that." He was on a white sofa, comfortable, a genial host. "But you didn't come here to talk about Marilyn, did you?"

"I'm looking for Nadja," I said.

"I haven't seen her all day."

"Have you talked with Bram Walker today?"

"Yeah I just called him," he said. "But, he hasn't seen Nadja either."

"When was that?"

"About an hour ago. Why?"

"I just wanted to ask her a couple of questions," I said. "Did Bram tell you Marilyn didn't want to deal drugs anymore?"

"Mr. Cramer, why do you meddle in other peoples' business?" He wasn't so genial now, but annoyed. "I don't mind a friendly visit. I enjoy company. But I don't like the way you interfere with other peoples' business."

"One of my bad habits, I guess. Where do you think I might find Nadja?"

"I told you, I don't know."

"Does she have an address?"

"You might try Bram's."

"Does Nadja know a small dark woman with short black hair?" I said. "About 30 or so?"

He stared at me, unsmiling. "You are persistent."

"Then you know her?" I countered.

"I know someone who fits that description," he said warily. "She's called the Princess."

"Princess?"

"She claims to be Russian nobility. I think it's funny. She's probably a runaway from Belarus or somewhere." He seemed to think that was amusing.

"Does she have a name?"

"We just call her the Princess. She lives at the Walton Arms. Third Avenue. In the tenth block. One of those ridiculous buildings."

I thanked him and left. He seemed glad to be rid of me. I think we both were.

The Walton Arms did look kind of ridiculous. An architect's chrome and glass monument to himself. There was a security guard who was busy yakking with a bleached blonde who had too much makeup. I walked into the small entry way, looked at the names on the mail boxes, and took a polished elevator up to the fifth floor.

The Princess was a lean and wiry woman, with opaque almond saucers for eyes. Almost Bedouin in appearance. She wore an off-white satin shirt and tailored black pants. There was an accent in her voice, but I couldn't quite place it. Could have been from one of the former Southern Republics. But what did I know? She looked me up and down, scornfully. "Vhat do you vant?" she snapped in a deep accent.

"I'd like to talk with Nadja," I said.

"She is not here."

"Okay. She's not here. Do you know where she is?"

"I do not know this. I have not seen her in ages."

"You drove her away from Bram Walker's place," I said. "Where did you take her?"

Her eyes went frigid. "I am afraid you are mistaken. Good bye."

As she was closing the door in my face, "It's okay, Princess," I heard Nadja say from inside the apartment. "Let him in. He knows Marilyn."

The Princess reluctantly let me inside. She smelled of jasmine. Nadja came out from a bedroom into the living room. She didn't look happy. "You saw me?" she said.

I sat down in an overstuffed chair. "Running away like that, doesn't look very good."

The Princess put her hands on her hips and shot daggers with her eyes at me. She looked at me and spoke to Nadja. "Who is this fool? Vhat does he vant here?"

"He's an accountant," Nadja said. "A forensic accountant, to be exact. He's working for Marilyn's grandfather. He must have seen me leaving Bram's apartment."

"You do not have to talk to this person," the Princess said. "I vill throw him out." The Princess took a step toward me.

"Look, don't try to …" I'd just about had it with this Princess.

"Oh, what am I going to do …" Nadja said hopelessly.

"Look, I want to talk to you alone," I told Nadja.

"I vill not leave here," the Princess said adamantly.

"Princess, please," Nadja pleaded. "You're not making this any easier."

The Princess stalked to a bedroom and shut the door firmly. I had no doubt she was pressing her ear to the other side of the door.

"Why don't you sit down for a minute?" I said to Nadja.

"I'd rather stand."

"Who's this Princess?"

" … A friend of mine."

"You were in Bram's apartment, weren't you?"

"You know I was."

"How long were you there?"

"Only a couple of minutes," she said. "Bram called me, told me he needed me to come over. He knew I was here with the Princess. She drove me over. When I got there, he was …"

"How long did you stay?"

"I saw he was dead. I, I, I was scared and ran out."

"You have any idea what he wanted?"

"No."

She was fingering her pearls. She wasn't ready to jump through hoops. But at least she was talking to me. That was definitely an improvement.

"You think he killed himself?"

She said it looked that way, but she didn't think so. "There is no reason for him to kill himself, and where did the gun come from? He didn't own a gun."

"Did he have an argument with Frank or someone else?" I asked.

She was surprised at the question. "They were best friends."

"You know they were dealing crack—and cutting it with wax, don't you?"

Nadja shrugged. "They needed money to live. It's hard. There's so many artists—especially here in New York. There's a lot of people who sell drugs on the street because they're desperate for money."

Maybe they should go to school and study to be accountants or auditors, so they can find good jobs, I thought. "Where did they get the stuff?"

"I don't know."

"Sergei Relgado?"

"I told you I don't know."

"Bram, Frank and Teddy. They were all artists, and they were all friends. Teddy's dead, and now Bram. Don't you think that's a little strange?"

"This isn't funny," she snapped.

"Darn right it's not funny."

"What do you want me to say?"

I leaned back and looked up at her. "Nadja, look. You're up to your eyeballs in this mess. The police will find out that you were his girlfriend, and eventually they'll catch up with you. What are you going to tell them?"

"I'll tell the truth. That I didn't have anything to do with it."

"You ran away. Somebody must have seen you. The police will find out. You're a suspect, Nadja. Tell me everything you know."

Just then the bedroom door burst open, and the Princess came charging across the room at me, her face contorted with rage. I bounced out of the chair to meet her head on. She clawed at my face and tried to kick me. I twisted my body so her foot landed square on the side of my knee. My leg buckled, and I dropped to the floor in pain. So much for the sedentary life style of a professor. I didn't know if I'd ever walk again.

Nadja kept screaming at the Princess to stop and succeeded in pulling her away.

I got to my feet and went into the bathroom to wash the blood from my face. I could hear Nadja and the Princess arguing with each other.

I went back into the living room. "Knock it off. Both of you. You want the neighbors to call the police?"

They stared at me, Nadja looking dumb, and the Princess glaring.

I said to Nadja, "What's her problem?" I jerked a thumb at the Princess. "Is she your mother?"

The Princess stared at me.

"Oh please," Nadja wailed.

I looked at Nadja. "Maybe you wanted out too, and Bram said no, so you killed him." I didn't really believe that. She didn't have a mighty grandfather to use as leverage on her. But it was something to say.

"Get out of here," the Princess ordered.

I left. My face hurt. Shaving was not going to be fun tomorrow morning.

# Ten

*Unless the firm recognizes differences in cost behavior among segments, there is a significant danger that incorrect or average-cost pricing will provide openings for competitors. Thus, cost analysis at the segment level must often supplement analysis at the business unit level.*

—Michael E. Porter

Tom was waiting for me at our accounting office. His gray suit coat was hung over the back of a chair, and he'd rolled up his white shirt sleeves. "Hot today," he said. "Where've you been? What happened to you?"

I told him.

"This thing gets crazier and crazier." He scratched his head. "I followed that blonde, Sandra, after she left the deli. Went to the Antalya Room, left there, alone, went to Grand Central. Took a train to Long Beach. I made sure she left with the train, then came back here."

"Two suicides, or two murders," I said. "Both drug dealers."

"Looks like somebody might be muscling into a territory," Tom said.

"Drug related hits?" I said. "Could be. I just don't think so. Their customers were probably all small-time."

"Yeah and hit men don't usually leave their weapons behind. But if they were drug related hits—my bet is on Sergei Relgado," Tom concluded.

"He fits in here some place. But where? The takt time for solving this engagement is not favorable" I said.

"Takt?" Tom looked confused.

"Takt time is the speed at which units must be manufactured to meet customer's demand. It's derived from the German word Taktzeit and translates as cycle time. Just a little humor." I smiled. "We could surely use it."

"Okay. Look, Sergei said you were suckered in," Tom looked at me. "Don't you see? You find two bodies. Two. Do you report either one? No. Ethics violations, Lenny—and slightly illegal. And what's your excuse? You're protecting your clients. Myra Riley. Lloyd Henderson. Privilege only exists for accountants in a few states, like Maryland, Louisiana, or Texas. And there's no federal privilege, Lenny. All you have is confidentiality with your clients here in New York. Only lawyers get the advocacy privilege—and that doesn't excuse breaking the law."

I was already ahead of Tom, but I let him go on. "If the police don't buy the suicide angle, then who's the fall guy? Who found the bodies? Who delivered the blackmail money? Who's been trying to keep everything quiet? Some coincidence. Why should the police buy some cockamamie story from you? Just protecting your clients. Right. By leaving the scene of two homicides and withholding evidence, you're a prime suspect. Your Ph.D. won't help you out on this one. If you'd go that far for your clients, why not more? Let's say the two rip-off, drug dealing artists were threatening your client somehow. So, you knocked them off for the sake of the client. A jury might decide that way. Sergei's got to be in on it, because he knew you were being set up. Either that, or he found out about it and had a reason for wanting to put you under his control. If that isn't being suckered in, I don't know what is."

Tom was no junior, green shade forensic accountant. He had street savvy and a clear head. He knew how to cut through the incessant smoke and mirrors.

"A good theory," I said. "It fits okay. But we still don't know *why* they were killed. Who'd they rip-off with the wax, and where's the payback? We don't even know who killed them. If your theory's right, then Lloyd Henderson's behind the whole thing. But what does he want? It can't be money. He's got more money than he knows what to do with."

"The more you have, the more you want."

I grabbed the phone and called Henderson. He was still in his office. I told him I'd be right over.

"Want me to go with you?" Tom asked.

"No. Marilyn and her friends were probably aggregating a lot of small sales of crack and laundering the cash proceeds for Relgado by staging the sale of a fake painting through her mother's gallery, and then using the money to make a 'loan repayment' back to Relgado. Why don't you go back to the art gallery and check the invoices for all the paintings purchased over the last two years. See if any came from the corpses, from Henderson, or from *any* other fishy sources. There must be a connection with the art forgery angle. Match the purchase invoices with the sales invoices and verify the related cash flows. Confirm the actual existence of any repeat-buyers and watch for big sales timed closely with repayments on Relgado's loan. Find out all the ways they are cooking the books. I'll call you after I see King Midas."

"Just don't fly off the handle," Tom cautioned. "He'll bury you if he thought you're going to stand in his way, and nobody will ever find you."

I thought out loud. "Could we use sensitivity analysis to solve this problem?" Sensitivity analysis is the "what if" process of altering certain key variables to assess the effect on the original outcome.

"What?" Tom almost shouted.

"Just a crazy thought. Forget it."

"You are too esoteric."

"Well, that's a big word." I smiled.

"If the shoe fits, wear it," Tom replied.

\* \* \*

Paul Manfred showed me to Henderson's office. He was silent as usual.

Lloyd Henderson was standing by a shelf full of books with brightly colored jackets. He had on a navy-blue suit. It was tailored like a movie star's. "What's the emergency, Dr. Cramer?"

"Another suicide," I said. I didn't bother to sit down. "Teddy Noren and now Bram Walker. Kind of strange, isn't it? Both were close to your granddaughter."

He moved to a chair and sat down with an expression that looked like a wise old Indian chief. "You think I know something about these deaths?"

"I wouldn't be surprised," I said.

"Sit down, Dr. Cramer."

I sat down.

"I did not engineer anyone's death, Doctor. You have my word on that. If you think I did, you're welcome to go to the police."

"I found a dead body, Bram Walker. I didn't report it again, because you want all of this handled quietly. The body's probably been found by now. If I go to the police now, they'll put thumb screws on my big toe until they get a confession. Both bodies looked like suicide. I don't buy it. I'm chasing financial shadows in the dark, and I don't like it. Maybe you can enlighten me."

"You think I hold strings and manipulate these little puppets?"

"That wouldn't surprise me either."

"If I wanted to kill people, why would I need you? I know enough people I could call upon to deal with any situation."

"Paul Manfred?"

His eyes twinkled. "Paul is my personal bodyguard."

"What about Sergei Relgado?"

"He's Sandra's problem."

"You know about them?" I was surprised.

"There is not much I don't know about my family, Dr. Cramer."

"Then what did you bring me in for?" I said almost irritated. Was Tom right with his theory? Was I just a sucker, being set up to take a fall for Henderson?

"I need you to find out what few things I don't already know about my family members' entanglements," he said. "My granddaughter is being used by someone to extort money from me. Money or something else. I'll not let my granddaughter be put in danger."

Henderson paused. "The 50 thousand dollars was no doubt a test. So far no one has contacted me looking for more money. Or anything else. I have three daughters. I despise them all. They do nothing but defy me. I let Myra go because she married beneath her. Old fashioned, yes, but she would not listen to me. I could see where it was headed. Sandra and Cora, they stay with me, but not because they have any love for me. They just want to make sure I don't write them out of my will. Greed sits on our shoulders, Doctor, all the time."

"Or something else," I said. "If it's not money, then what is it? I've got a feeling you know what it is."

"It probably has to do with the new microchip my people are developing, Dr. Cramer. A new type of memory that will revolutionize the industry. There are a lot of people who stand to lose a lot of money when we come on line with it. It has extensive defense system applications."

"Maybe."

He laughed hollowly. "You don't believe me? Well, that's irrelevant. You're on my payroll. I don't have to worry about what you think of me. Your partner John Grant, he's also greedy. I'm paying him well for your forensic services."

I wondered if he knew about Sandra and Paul Manfred. If he didn't, then it might be a jolt. But where would it get me to just pander their gossip? He was talking. But was it worth a nickel?

We didn't shake hands when I left. Paul Manfred saw me out. Two state police officers and a detective were waiting for me at my accounting office.

Bram Walker's body had been found. Two people who knew Nadja swore they'd seen her running from the building. They'd tracked her down to the Princess, and she admitted being there. The Princess stuck in her two cents and told the police I'd been in the apartment, and then came to question Nadja. So now the police were here, and they weren't too polite. They were ready to drag me off to the nearest police station for some heavy questioning when John Grant rushed a few phone calls. He did have some valuable connections. The police officers were steamed, because they didn't like the interference from upstairs. But at least they lost their enthusiasm for taking me down to the jail house.

While the police officers were on my neck with questions, their ballistics lab checked the murder weapon. No fingerprints, but the gun was registered to Paul Manfred.

Two detectives went to Henderson's office, but Manfred was nowhere to be found. He had disappeared. Who tipped him off? His description was in the late edition of the local newspaper, and on the next TV cable news broadcasts.

Manfred's story came on right after the headline news, about some Hazirian Liberation Army—extremists demanding the complete withdrawal of U.S. military presence from Iraq and Afghanistan. They were giving us 10 days to comply, or they would blow up the Social Security Administration buildings in Baltimore. Ten days. How generous of them. Even if they blew those buildings with nobody in them, the loss of those computers would throw the livelihoods of tens of millions of people into chaos. The commentator said

National Security Agency people believed they were following a trail from Baghdad, through eastern Turkey. Then up through Azerbaijan and into the Republic of Georgia. From there they were making it into Canada, then finding ways to come down into the U.S. But how did these guys get into the U.S.? I wondered. Maybe they just get tourist visas.

The police left, but not before I persuaded them to take one of our junior practice associates along. That is, I persuaded them with John Grant's help. I told him to stay put in Police Plaza and keep his eyes and ears opened, while I stayed in my office.

Hildy wanted to stay, but I told her to go home for the day. Tom brought dinner for two, from a burger place, and we ate à la carte in my office.

I told our junior in police headquarters to check in every half-hour.

He did.

Through the night the reports came in from people who'd spotted Paul Manfred. It was like hearing Elvis sightings.

He'd been seen in the Silk Stocking District, Chelsea, the Village, Brooklyn Heights, Flatbush, Rego Park, Woodhaven, Ozone Park, Orange, New Jersey, Great Neck, Staten Island, and Penn Station.

"It seems like he's been seen everywhere but Bangkok," I told Tom.

"How did he know the law was after him?"

"Maybe he got a message from the Invisible Man," I said.

"You think Johnny Depp did it?"

"I don't know what to think. Why would Manfred kill somebody with his own gun, then leave it behind?" I said. "It just doesn't make sense."

"Nothing in this crazy engagement makes sense," Tom concluded. "You going to stay here all night?"

"I don't know. But I'd sure like to ask Paul Manfred a few questions right now. Let's hope the police will let me talk to him when they find him."

"With all the connections Grant pulls out of the woodwork, they'll probably deliver him to you by FedEx, and have you sign-off for him."

"He really came through for me, didn't he?"

"I'm as blown away as you are," Tom yawned. "But what else could he do? He had to protect his people. He can't afford not to in this business."

It was getting to be the middle of the night and the streets were unusually quiet. The moon was only a sliver. Cold. Impersonal. Like a round gray haze. Tom took the next phone call, and grimaced. He put down the receiver. "Somebody called the police to inform them he remembers seeing someone who looks like Manfred buying a fishing pole in Howard Beach."

"What else? This is New York."

"You get every imaginable crank calling in when something like this turns up. I'm beat. I've got to sack out for a while. Where is that old cot they keep stored around here?"

* * *

In the dawn's early light, the city looked somber. A haze of amber fog tinted the air. But slowly the city started coming to life again. Little by little the traffic began picking up. That's when I really started to feel it. The paws of exhaustion. Mental, emotional, and physical. When Hildy walked in I told her I was going home.

Tom was up and around. "Let's have breakfast."

"I hate morning people. I need to crash."

"You look like you need it—some breakfast might help."

I ignored him and went home.

It was noon when a call from Myra woke me. Her voice had an edge like acid. "What's going on? I've had police everywhere here."

"They're looking for Paul."

"I know. But why me?" I could imagine her eyes.

"Why not? Paul worked for your father. They're probably just questioning all the family members."

"They've been harassing Sandra," Myra said. "Why her? How did they know she and Paul went out together?"

"I don't know."

"You didn't tell them—"

"Not about that. It's a crazy case. They're probably just as stumped as I am."

"Can you come here for lunch?"

"Lunch? I haven't had breakfast yet."

"I need to see you."

"I'll come over in a couple of hours." I hung up. Shaved, very carefully, and took a hot steaming shower. I felt livelier than a corpse, but not by much. I dressed and went out into a drizzle. This whole engagement was starting to remind me of the time I inventoried equipment in a hospital morgue. It was my first job as a junior accounting staff member.

All the computerized depreciation records for the hospital had to be verified by checking tag numbers on the entire hospital's inventory of major moveable capital equipment—including the equipment in the morgue. They had to allocate depreciation expense to appropriate departments somehow. It was important for cost reimbursement, based on step-down allocation worksheets.

Step-down allocations are used to assign the costs of service departments—like data processing, fiscal administration, and medical records—to revenue producing departments like radiology, clinical pathology, operating room, and ICU. The step-down method gets its name from the way the numbers are arranged on the worksheet. They sort of step down like a staircase. The method is like a "slinky" moving down the steps picking up lint (costs) from each step. It's one of the few aesthetic things we do in accounting. I usually illustrate it for my students with a chart.

STEP-DOWN ALLOCATION WORKSHEET

Like I said, the numbers step down. Allocating service department costs to revenue producing departments allows a full cost measure for the services that are sold. The ability of each marketable service to cover all its direct and indirect costs, and produce a profit, can be assessed by comparing its revenues to these full costs.

Unbelievably, step-down allocation worksheets have been used by Medicare for years, to allocate hundreds of billions of dollars in healthcare payments to hospitals throughout the country. Why did they choose the step-down method? Why not use the direct method, or the reciprocal method? Probably because its halfway in between. Better than direct, and not as complicated as reciprocal. A political compromise no doubt. Why not some other method? Just think how accountants changed the massive flow of public resources for 30 plus years, just by selecting a cost allocation method. But, then again, step-down worksheets do have a certain eye appeal.

| | Data Processing | Fiscal Admin. | Medical Records | Radiology | Clinical Pathology | Operating Room | TOTAL |
|---|---|---|---|---|---|---|---|
| **Direct costs:** | $30,000 | $20,000 | $10,000 | $100,000 | $50,000 | $80,000 | $290,000 |
| **D.P. Allocation:*** | (30,000) | 1,000 | 1,500 | 10,000 | 8,000 | 9,500 | |
| | $0 | $21,000 | | | | | |
| **F.A. Allocation:*** | | (21,000) | 1,200 | 7,000 | 6,000 | 6,800 | |
| | | $0 | $12,700 | | | | |
| **M.R. Allocation:*** | | | (12,700) | 4,400 | 4,000 | 4,300 | |
| | | | $0 | | | | |
| **Total:** | | | | $121,400 | $68,000 | $100,600 | $290,000 |

*Assumes allocations based on appropriate allocation base for service.

Yes, that same blah, feeling—like lifting a corner of the draped sheet over a stiff on a gurney, so I could check the tag number by his foot. Just blah. It was in the walk-in freezer. Then check the autopsy tables, tools. Hmm. Maybe that first assignment is what got me interested in forensic accounting. Yes, a cost accounting professor can be a forensic accountant. A great deal of forensic accounting deals with some type of allocation. That's a morbid thought. Blame it all on step-down cost allocation worksheets for depreciation reimbursement of a morgue.

* * *

When I arrived at Myra's apartment, she had coffee perking. I drank it and had some scrambled eggs. Then she told me Sandra had been there to see her.

"Did she tell you where Paul is?"

Myra frowned. "No. How would she know? He's probably hiding somewhere—or maybe he's even left the country." She was eating a tuna fish sandwich and fruit salad.

"Do you think he's hiding in that big house on the Island?"

"The police were there with a warrant. They didn't find him. My father wouldn't hide a criminal, even if it was Paul," she said.

"We don't really know if he is a criminal do we," I said. "Not counting his past record, that is."

"What does that mean?"

I had a second cup of coffee. It wasn't bad. "It means even though it was his gun, I doubt he did the shooting."

"I don't get it."

"Maybe somebody took Paul's gun, shot Walker, and intentionally left the gun behind to frame your father's bodyguard."

"But why?"

"I told you. To frame him." My patience was starting to wear thin.

"I mean, why Paul?"

"He's got a record. He's a made to order patsy. A perfect fall guy."

"But—" She bit her lip.

"Also," I said. "His gun? Where did he keep his gun? In your father's house, I guess. Who could get it? Someone in your family?"

"You mean Sandra?"

"Sandra … or your father."

"Sandra was close to Paul. And why should my father frame Paul? Paul's been loyal to him."

"Would he be so fond of Paul if he found out Paul was having an affair with Sandra?"

Myra seemed confused. So was I. Even though her father kicked her out, Myra probably still felt some family loyalty. But I could be wrong. There are many people who hate their relatives. Fathers, mothers, brothers, and sisters. Sons and daughters. In-laws, and outlaws. Lloyd Henderson told me he despised his own daughters. Maybe the feeling was mutual. Sounds like a great family.

"Since you mentioned Sandra," Myra said, "what about Cora? Isn't she a suspect too?"

"So far she's the invisible woman. Either she's oblivious to all of this, or she's extremely clever."

"Well Cora has always been distant. I never could get close to her. I tried. I thought I reached Sandra for a while, and then it's like she puts up a wall, and that was the end of it. I always hated living in that house. You could just feel the ice growing on the walls. My parents had a bitter marriage. My mother died fairly young. I still think about my mother. What she must have gone through — although she had her calculating moments too."

Myra wanted me to stay, but I couldn't. I took my leave, and I went back to the office.

Tom had been talking to Shirley, the waitress from the Antalya Room, Sergei Relgado's joint. He had gone to have breakfast with her. "I told her my life's story. Then she told me her life's story. That exhausted both of us. We had a nice time," Tom related.

"I can imagine."

"Listen, this kid keeps her ears open," Tom said. "That Sandra babe, who's Jeannette when she's got her wig on, well, according to Shirley, she and Sergei are no lovers. In fact, she thinks Sergei hates her guts."

"That's why Sergei likes to show her off? That's what Sandra told me."

"No." Tom shook his head. "Shirley thinks it's all an act. She thinks Sandra has some leverage on Relgado, and Relgado has to play along. That's what Shirley thinks anyway."

"That might answer a few questions," I said. "If Shirley's right."

Tom grinned at me. "You're thinking outside the box again."

"We know Relgado wouldn't go for small time stuff, like a fifty-thousand-dollar blackmail stunt. But what if Sandra had something big on him? What if Sandra's forcing him to go along with some scheme she and Manfred cooked up? That would answer a lot of questions."

Tom shook his head. "If Sandra had something on Sergei, he'd just knock her off—make her disappear quietly."

"Blackmailers are too sharp for that," I told Tom. "They cover their bases—keep long letters in safe deposit boxes, or hand them over to their lawyers with instructions to open up envelopes, in case they meet with suspicious accidents."

"As they say on *Criminal Minds*, who is the unsub? You think Sandra decided to get rid of Paul because she wanted everything for herself? Whatever it is they're after."

"I don't know," I said. "Paul could always blow the whistle if he thought Sandra was turning on him—unless Paul Manfred wasn't in on anything, and Sandra thinks she's playing every side against the middle for herself."

"But what's she after?" Tom asked. "Fifty-thousand bucks is nothing compared to her half of her father's estate."

Hildy walked into the room, and we bounced a few ideas off her. We really didn't get anywhere.

Our junior at Police Plaza called again. No crank calls for hours. No calls at all about Paul Manfred. I told him to go home and get some rest.

"The novelty must be wearing off," I told Tom.

"I'd like to know who it was that tipped Manfred off that the police were coming."

"There's always a back door," I said to Tom. He stood up.

"Do you need me to work tonight?" He asked.

"I guess I can spare you."

"Some people work regular hours you know."

"Got a date with Shirley?" I razzed.

"Yes. She's off tonight. I'm mixing a little business with pleasure. Between heart throbs I'll ask her about our pal Sergei. Shirley isn't too keen on him. She must fend him off from time to time. He's a slime."

"Right. She's just waiting for a billionaire like you to come along and sweep her off her feet in a romantic moment."

Tom pretended to be hurt and left.

I went home, packed, and took an afternoon flight to Dallas-Fort Worth. A taxi took me to the Green Oaks Inn, just off I-30. I met Rick Mannino at 9:00 in the Feather's restaurant in the hotel. It had a dance floor and a sunken bar in the middle. Rick Mannino was my contact at General Dynamics Corporation, a defense contractor with more than 98,000 employees in the Fort Worth area, with at least thirty billion dollars in world-wide sales.

Mannino outlined our expert witness strategy. "Look we have a number of different projects in our Fort Worth plant. Some are based on fixed price contracts and others are based on cost-plus. We have a security department that costs about $16 million a year. How do you think it should it be allocated to our different contracts?"

Mannino paused and smiled briefly. He was about six-feet-four and weighed about 190 pounds. He had a full head of dirty blond hair. "Of course, the Air Force would like the total $16 million to be allocated to the fixed price contracts—like our Soviet MIG flight simulator project. We'd rather allocate it to the cost-plus contracts—like our night pulse-laser sighting system."

Of course, on a military cost-plus contract, costs are reimbursed, and a fixed percentage profit is added on top. The higher the cost, the bigger the reimbursement, the more the profit. I thought back to my surrealistic accounting dream, and the CASBs role in regulating these cost allocation issues. "So, my job was to testify on the proper allocation of security department costs for your contracts in progress? With the break-up of the Soviet Union, why are you building a MIG flight simulator?"

"Right for the first question. For the second, many of the breakaway republics are still unstable. Plus, the Commonwealth—Russia—desperately needs the money. They're selling bad stuff to countries like India, and some in the Middle East that are still hostile to us. Even India and Pakistan have the bomb now. The next world war may not be as far off as we'd like to think. Now suppose I let you go get some rest, and I'll pick you up in the morning about 8:00. We'll tour some of the plants and let you ask questions. I'm sure the defense department lawyers are going to ask you if you've ever even been in one of our plants."

"You bet!"

After Mannino said goodbye, I went to the fifth floor and passed out cold for the night on the surprisingly comfortable hotel bed.

On Friday morning Mannino took me on the promised tour of the Fort Worth General Dynamics facilities. There were at least 20 buildings, with a mile-long assembly plant. Uniformed security guards were stationed everywhere, many of them carried fully automatic rifles. Throughout the day I referred to my blue copy of *Government Contract Guidebook*, by D.P. Arnauas and W.J. Ruberry.

Each of the several ways of reasonably allocating the security costs were based on a different cost driver (an activity that caused the cost), such as

  1. *floor space in the buildings*

  2. *the amount of labor cost of the projects*

  3. *direct engineering hours*

  4. *direct manufacturing labor hours*

  5. *number of employees*

  6. *accumulated total cost of the projects*

From Federal Acquisition Regulations (FAR) Subpart 31.2, I studied the definition of allocability, while I ate my $3.50 hamburger in one of the big cafeterias at General Dynamics:

A cost is allocable if it is assignable or chargeable to one or more cost objectives on the basis of relative benefits received or other equitable relationship. Subject to the foregoing, a cost is allocable to a Government contract if it:

  (a) *Is incurred specifically for the contract;*

  (b) *Benefits both the contract and other work, and can be distributed to them in reasonable proportion to the benefits received; or*

*(c) Is necessary to the overall operation of the business, although a direct relationship to any particular cost objective cannot be shown.*

I spent some time reviewing my Standard Form 1411, which includes cost or pricing data submitted to the federal government. I tentatively concluded that the cost of security should be allocated to the various projects, based on relative direct engineering hours—the activity that appeared best correlated with security costs.

Mannino indicated that the Air Force usually preferred allocations based on relative direct manufacturing labor costs. That keeps their costs relatively lower when their projects have considerably more engineering costs. Although the direct engineering costs can be added to the project costs itself, there are less general overhead costs allocated to the project using those direct manufacturing labor costs rather than engineering hours.

Around 5:30 Mannino and I passed through the security checkpoints and walked to his car. "They check everybody and everything. They even check your lunch thermos. We had an employee one time that used his thermos to smuggle out components of our smart bomb guidance system. By taking a few chips and circuits at a time, over the course of a year he almost stole enough to blow our whole program—before he got caught, that is," Mannino said.

Mannino had two tickets to see a Rangers game. On the way to Arlington stadium, we passed the University of Texas at Arlington on Cooper and Mitchell streets. And along the way I noticed a business called "4 Day Tire Store." Why would a tire store want to close for three days out of every week?

Mannino stopped at a Texas Commerce Bank ATM on Border Street, to get some cash. A Honda in front of the ATM had a bumper sticker that said, "Backing the Blue," referring to the police, and another one, "Support Beef. Run Over a Chicken."

On the way to a restaurant near the Ballpark in Arlington, we were stopped at a railroad crossing for a fast-moving train. "I knew a train engineer once who fell asleep and ran a mile-long coal train through a stop signal—was a miracle nobody got killed. Some engineers tie down the dead man switch so they can sleep on long hauls. Control system override. Scary. It's a foot pedal that's supposed to trigger the brakes in case the engineer has a heart-attack or something. So much for the control system," I reported like an auditor assessing risk.

Mannino told a few "war stories" of his own.

From the steps of the restaurant I could see the Ballpark at Arlington. Mannino proudly said that Nolan Ryan finished out his career with the Rangers. He pitched seven no-hitters and had a 10-year contract before he retired. I once saw him pitch a no-hitter.

"What a pitching arm," I said graciously, mustering my social skills, as we sat down and looked at the menus.

"You know that George Bush, Jr. at one time was part owner of the Texas Rangers," Mannino said.

"Didn't I read that George Bush's Presidential library is built at SMU in Dallas."

"Right," Mannino replied. "The senior Bush's library is in College Station."

At that point our waiter arrived and gave us some Mardi Gras beads. I ordered Cajun crawfish bisque, red beans and rice, and sausage. Mannino told me that a Cajun was a Louisiana native descended from French speaking immigrants from Acadia. The food was pretty good—hot and spicy.

After we finished eating we moved Mannino's car from the restaurant to the stadium parking lot. We walked toward the stadium. It was hot—6:30 P.M. and still 96 degrees. As we got close to the massive Ranger-red brick and granite exterior of the stadium, I saw the façade was wrapped with bas reliefs of longhorn cattle, and scenes from the state's history. There were stories of the Alamo, the oil boom, and the space program.

It was an outdoor stadium, with real Bermuda and rye grass on the field. Mannino said the stadium can hold 48,000 fans. It slowly filled up all the way, because the Rangers were in a tight race for first place in their division. In right field there was a huge banner with a "34" on it. Mannino said number 34 was Nolan Ryan's retired number.

The first wave started in the second inning, but by the third inning the Rangers' pitcher didn't come back out. He left because he had a sore arm. When the Toronto Blue Jays were five runs ahead, I started looking around at the signs in the stadium—Dr. Pepper, Delta the Orient, Well Made Weller Made, and Enjoy Coca-Cola, among others. There were jets flying over from DFW airport. Someone had a homemade sign: "Mazara You're The One." They were referring to Normar Mazara, nicknamed Big Chill.

Soon my biggest thrill was hearing the hot-dog man bark "Hot dog." Mannino said he was one of a kind. "Sounds like the Hunch Back of Notre Dame," I said. I was erudite.

During the sixth inning there was a dot race. Three different colored dots raced around the score board. Sponsored by Whataburger. My yellow dot card had a chance to win. Oh boy.

For some reason the racing dots started going so fast they looked like they were moving backward. It reminded me of backflush costing. With the just-in-time inventory systems at some companies, the elapsed time between receipt of raw materials, and the production of the finished goods is drastically reduced. Work-in-process becomes a trivial amount. So, a retrospective cost estimate of the fast-moving work-in process inventory is considered good enough, for financial reporting.

Back flushing accumulates costs by working backward, through the accounting information after high speed production is completed. High speed production—yes, it's not suitable with long involved complex production process. The completion of the product or its sale is considered a trigger point for assigning costs. You work backwards from the end of the accounting period, by using end-of-period estimates of the material and conversion of all the unfinished goods. You accumulate all the costs through the end of the period and make adjustments, if needed or material, to unfinished goods. Wait until the end to see what there is. The red dot won the race. Too bad. I lost.

"Where do they find blue gloves?" Mannino asked. "Do they cost more than normal gloves?" Several of the Blue Jays' players wore blue gloves.

"Well, like I tell my students, when cows go to the slaughter house, they use everything but the 'moo.'"

"The what?"

"The 'moo.' 'Moo.' They can't sell the 'moo.' The cow goes in one end, and the steak, hamburger, prime rib, tallow for soap-making, cow hide for baseball gloves and baseballs, all come out the other end. They even use the blood. It's a joint-cost allocation problem."

"They sell the blood to vampires," Mannino smiled. "I believe I saw a movie where most of the people were vampires, and they were running out of human blood. How do they price all those products?" he asked.

"I missed that movie. That's a good question. There's a lot of costs that result in a lot of products. Just like the oil business. You really want to know?"

"Sure." He was bored with the game too.

"Joint costs can be allocated using physical measurements. For example, in the oil industry you can use BTUs."

"But a pound of prime rib costs much more than hamburger," Mannino protested.

"Right. There's four alternative methods that are favored by most companies — the net-realizable value method, the constant gross margin percentage method, the sales value at split-off method, and the physical units at split-off method."

"Oh no, I feel a lecture coming." Just then the crowd started shouting, because Elvis Andrus hit a home run.

"For the alternative methods, we go to the marketplace and work backward. The net-realizable value is calculated by taking the selling price, less the costs of completion for sales occurring after the split-off point."

"Split-off point?"

"The point where the joint products can be separately identified, and where the decision to sell or process any of them further can be made independently of the other products. The joint costs are then allocated based upon this net-realizable value."

"Hot dogs. Hot dogs," the Hunchback of Notre Dame barked hoarsely as he shuffled by us. I took a paper napkin and drew my usual simplified, split-off point diagram for analyzing joint cost problems.

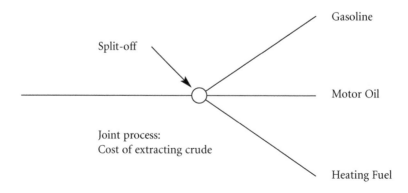

"In the classroom I use the arm, wrist, palm, and fingers for this example. You can stop at the first knuckle or go to the fingernail."

"In a similar fashion, if raw products can be sold at the split-off point to other processors, the joint costs can be allocated to the different products based upon relative sales value, or physical units, at the split-off point. Then again, we could just calculate the gross margin percentage for all the joint products taken together. Then we could impute that percentage back on each of the individual products—giving them all the same gross margin rate. Next we would just plug the allocation of joint cost that we need to make it work."

"Okay. So, which is best?" Mannino asked.

"Like all the allocation methods, in the final analysis each one is an arbitrary choice, based on implicit assumptions. But a lot of managers favor the net-realizable-value method. It's based on the economic contribution of the joint products to coverage of common, or joint costs. Unlike the physical units and sales value at split off methods, it requires assumptions about the company's choice to process further or not and requires estimates for the costs of further processing. Actually, it's my favorite."

"All right, try this on," Mannino grinned. "I have a mint, 1968 Nolan Ryan rookie baseball card. The last time I checked it was worth about $22,000. Trouble is that one-half of the card is Jerry Koosman. Koosman pitched for 19 years, won 222 games, but he is no Hall of Fame material. My question is, how do I allocate my $800 cost of the card between Koosman and Ryan?"

"One baseball card worth 22,000 bucks?" I repeated, as I was thinking. "Why don't you get a good pair of scissors and cut the card in half?" I smiled broadly.

Mannino groaned, even though he knew I was kidding. "Nolan says that Jerry Koosman keeps reminding him that Koosman's Mets rookie card keeps climbing in value. One sold for $36,000. By the way, a mint Mickey Mantle rookie card has sold for as much as $2.88 million at auction."

"Must be a form of art," I concluded flatly. "My mother threw all of my baseball cards away. Maybe they were sunk costs."

"That's what everyone says," Mannino replied.

# Eleven

*Responsibility accounting means that each sale or cost that a company expects during a year is delegated to a department manager and should appear in a departmental budget. The total revenues and costs in all the departmental revenue and expense budgets should equal the total budgeted revenues and costs for the company for the coming year.*

—Thomas E. Lynch

The afternoon when I returned to the "Big Apple," John Maple, a homicide detective, called on me. The drizzle outside had long since stopped, and now it was getting cold. Definitely a contrast to the hot weather in Texas. The detective sat across from me. He was young. Built like a bull. He had a square face with a prominent nose. His hair was dark black, combed straight back, with waves in it. He didn't look very happy.

"We've been putting two and two together," he said. "There has to be a connection between Walker and Teddy Noren. They knew each other, and they were found dead the same way. We're ruling out the suicide angle in Noren's death. Two murders. Same M.O. Probably by the same person. We're looking for Paul Manfred because the gun found with Walker was registered to his name. But that doesn't mean he killed both, or even one of them."

A very smart police officer, I thought.

We traded glances and suddenly he grinned. It made him look boyish. But he still wasn't my best friend. He was about thirty-ish, and his face was tanned. "You're in the middle of this, Dr. Cramer. You may not have killed anyone, but you haven't told us everything you know."

"I told you what I know."

"You know where Paul Manfred is now?"

"No. Wish I did."

"Do you think Manfred killed these two guys?"

"No. I think he's being framed."

"What makes you think that?"

"I just think it."

"Not good enough."

Heavy silence, thick as pea soup.

"Why did you go to see Myra Riley last Thursday?" he asked.

So, I'd been followed. "I don't like eating alone."

His face went grim. "Wrong answer."

"I asked her a couple of questions. But the answers weren't worth much."

"That's not what I call a lot of cooperation," he said.

"If something comes up, I'll call you."

"That's nice of you," he retorted.

The sarcasm didn't affect me at all. I can take it. An expert witness must have thick skin when testifying in the courtroom. Attorneys are not the nicest people in the courtroom.

"We have a murder case on our hands, and no cooperation from anyone. Two murders. This Lloyd Henderson is one of those big shots we can't touch, because he's got a small army of lawyers to shield him. Your boss, Grant, has got connections with the D.A.'s office, so I'm told we have to handle you carefully. It is enough to make me want to quit."

"Grant is my partner. I'm a professor. I'm only doing a favor for the President of my university."

He stood up, frustrated. A strong detective, maybe untarnished, with a healthy contempt for people who get away with things, especially culpable people with political pull. He didn't say good-bye. He turned and walked out. Left me his card.

Tom called a half hour later. "Shirley's got a friend," he said.

"Not interested," I sighed.

"We could have dinner together. Maybe go to a movie."

"I don't feel like eating. I don't feel like a movie. I need to get a decent night's sleep tonight." I told him about the visit from the homicide detective. I told him about the tail he'd put on me.

"You think the phone is tapped?"

"I don't think so," I said. "Hildy would never let anyone into this office without asking me first."

"You're in the dark ages, Lenny. The boys have equipment now you wouldn't believe."

"Okay. What can I do?"

"I think you should come with us. But first, make sure your shadow gets lost."

"Where do we meet?"

"Columbus Circle. I'll pick you up in an hour."

"Yes, but—"

Tom hung up.

If I was being followed, then this time it was by an expert. I used a bus, a subway, and a cab. Tom picked me up at Columbus Circle. There was no one in the car with him.

"I don't think I was followed. If I was, I must have lost him."

"Two men in cars and one man on foot. They're still with you, Lenny."

"What? Oh well. What do you expect? I'm an accountant, not a detective."

"Well the police seem to think you're fairly important. Doesn't that make you feel great? You have a police escort."

"Think we can we lose them?"

"You don't think I'd embarrass Shirley and her friend by showing up with a parade of detectives on our tail, do you?"

"Who is this friend anyway?"

"You don't know her," Tom said. "But she's a talker." He cut into Central Park. "We don't have to worry about the guy on foot now. One of the cars picked him up."

"Oh, now I can breathe easier," I said.

"Give me a break," Tom said. He came out on Fifth Avenue. "Now I'll show you how an expert does it."

It wasn't going to be easy, because the cars no doubt had radio contact. They weren't going to call in the Marines because we weren't wanted for anything. This was strictly a surveillance job. No roadblocks or anything dramatic. Still—two cars. One car wouldn't be too hard. But two of them. Well, Tom was good at tailing people, and I suppose at losing tails, when he wanted to lose them.

We headed east for Lexington, then downtown to 14th Street, then down the row of blocks where all the book stores are huddled together like the garment district. Down Broadway, past City Hall, into the Wall Street area.

By now the police had to know we were trying to lose them. Throwing caution to the wind, one of the cars inched forward. I thought he was going to climb into our hip pockets.

Then Tom did something cute. He made a fast-right turn and our back-hugging car kept on going. He'd circle the block and join the parade again, but Tom made another right, and then a left, and by that time with the semi-gridlock that was developing around us, the driver of the car would never catch up. That left us with just one tail.

"Do I get a raise?" Tom asked.

"I'm only second in command," I reminded him. "Way beyond my pay grade."

"I'm knocking myself out for nothing," Tom kidded.

I knew he was enjoying the challenge, as dubious as this little escapade was. "Watch out for red lights," I told him. "That's all we need."

"Those red lights better watch out for me." Tom double backed and soon we were on Park Row. "We are going to be late for our date, but I can't help it." Tom swung onto the Brooklyn Bridge.

He made a turn onto another lane and hung on. When we got off the bridge he pulled a U-turn and went back onto it, and we headed back into Manhattan. He drove through Chinatown, then Little Italy. "We lose them?"

I looked back. "I think so." But what did I know?

Her name was Shirley Mowen, and her friend was an administrative assistant named Stella Benson. They were waiting for us and were getting hungry. Stella was in her mid-20s, with reddish hair that hung like a thick satin curtain down her shoulders. She had innocent features and a soft, smooth face, almost almond shaped eyes.

We went to Peng Teng for dinner. We had the family dinner for four. "I just love Chinese food," Stella bubbled. Her voice was squeaky.

After finishing everything off with green tea and almond cookies, Tom said to Stella, "Tell my professor friend here about the Princess and Nadja."

So that's why Tom wanted me to join them.

"Oh, no," Stella pouted. "I'm not a blabbermouth."

"He's interested," Tom said.

"There's nothing to tell," Stella said, pouring tea for herself. "I met the Princess through Nadja. At a party. She asked me if I wanted to smoke a rock, and I was insulted. I told Shirley about it. When you asked Shirley if she knew anything about Nadja or the Princess, she remembered what I told her."

"Come on, Stella," Shirley urged. "Tell them the rest."

Stella flared up. "What are you trying to get me to say?"

People were staring. "Let's drop it," I said. "It can't be that important."

After some more small talk, Stella began easing her defenses a little. Well, she'd sold some rocks for them after all. It seemed that the Princess did most of the recruiting, and Bram Walker and Frank Masters were intermediaries who supplied the drugs. Yes. Stella had met Marilyn and Teddy. Marilyn was one of the street dealers, and Teddy did some weighing—and sometimes cutting, with chunks of wax. It was one of Sergei Relgado's rackets all right. She was sure of that. She also heard that Teddy and Marilyn were worried about something, and they were looking for someone else to front them the drugs instead. But nobody could just quit Relgado. Unless it was feet first.

"Did they ever try to sell any forged paintings," I inquired.

"How am I supposed to know that?" she squealed.

They decided on Times Square for a movie.

While the women went to the restroom, Tom and I talked in the lobby. "Might just turn out to be a hit by someone who found out he bought a bag of wax," Tom said. "Teddy Noren's murder, anyway."

"But what if Relgado had Teddy killed," I said, "then Bram Walker ..."

"Are we getting anywhere?"

"We know Relgado's behind the drug operation. Is he into art forgeries? Does he use them to launder the money through Myra's gallery? I don't think either one of us would be shocked. But why put the bite on Lloyd Henderson? What's he got to do with it? Relgado's rackets are big money. What in the world is fifty thousand to him? And why Henderson?"

"You think Relgado framed Paul Manfred?"

"If he did, he had help. Sandra-Jeannette, I'll bet."

"Sandra sneaks the gun out of her old man's house, gives it to Sergei, and one of Sergei's thugs blows Walker away."

"It makes some sense."

The two women joined us again, and we went to see the movie. Stella's perfume smelled like a flower shop. I felt content, and we laughed at the funny lines. It was a comedy. At this point I could use some comic relief.

We dropped them off at their homes, called it a night, and headed back.

* * *

The next morning, I got to the office on time for a change. Two messages were waiting for me. Or rather a phone number on each message. With just the initial, "P."

I took the two slips of paper downstairs with me and called him on my cell phone. I recognized Paul Manfred's voice. "Is it okay to talk?" he said.

"I'm in the lobby of my office building on my cell phone. No police with me."

"Henderson told me to call you."

"Call me? What do you want?"

"What do I want? I want out of here. I don't need this murder rap."

"Where do you wish to meet?"

"How about Washington Square Park? Under the arch?"

"In an hour?"

"Yeah." He hung up. And I hung up.

I decided not to go back upstairs. I called Hildy and told her to tell Tom to stay ready. Twenty minutes later I was in Washington Square Park. Under the arch, I waited three or four minutes before Manfred showed up. He was wearing a faded denim jacket with fringe, blue jeans, and he needed a shave. He wore a Mets' cap and sunglasses. We walked to a bench and sat down. The sun was out. Looked like it was going to be nice for the rest of the day.

"Who put the law on me?" he asked.

"How am I supposed to know?"

"You didn't bring the police," he said. "I've been watching you from Fifth Avenue. I can't trust anybody. Even old man Henderson. Cheap rat. He won't even get me a lawyer. He just told me to call you."

"When did you talk to him?"

"Early this morning." Paul Manfred didn't look too good. There were dark lines cutting into his cheeks below his sunglasses. "Rich old computer man, and that's all he can do for me."

"You want to talk about it?"

"Yeah. But I don't know who killed Bram Walker. And I don't know how they got my gun."

"I don't believe that," I said.

"I got a couple of ideas. It's Sandra or the old man."

"You're sure?"

"Gotta be."

"You just said you didn't know how the killer got your gun. Now you say it was Sandra or Lloyd Henderson."

"I still say it. The gun was in my locked briefcase, and I have the only key."

"So, the gun was taken after the case was forced open," I finished.

"My briefcase wasn't forced open. But Sandra could have done it. She could have used my key when I was sleeping."

"If that's how it was done, then that means this set-up was planned. But I can't see Sandra working on her own. What's behind this anyway? I want to know. Two artists get murdered. Somebody puts the bite on your boss for fifty thousand dollars. Marilyn Riley gets mixed up in some petty drug dealing racket. I find a forged painting. You get framed for murder — maybe by Sandra. What's the connection, Manfred?"

"I got the fifty thousand," Paul Manfred said.

I almost fell off the park bench. "What? How the — how did you get that?"

Paul grinned, but there was nothing funny about it. "Sandra and I did the blackmail letters. I'm telling' you this because I need your help. But if you tell anybody, I'll deny every word of it."

"Okay," I said. "But you know it's taxable income."

Paul just shook his head. "Blackmail's one thing, but murder's something' else. I am not gonna be no fall guy for Sandra, and I ain't going to be one for Relgado neither. I won't pay no taxes."

"How does Relgado fit into this thing? What in the world is fifty thousand to someone like Relgado anyway?"

"Nothing'. But 50 grand is 50 grand to *me*. The old man paid me nothing. Room and board. I figured 50 grand would pay for everything I put up with from that jerk. Sandra helped me. It wasn't the money for her. She and Cora do not like the old man. We knew about Marilyn and the drugs. Sandra found out from Sergei. She put on a wig and went out with him for kicks. I think she's got a couple of screws loose from living in that house so long. It's Relgado's operation. He thought it was funny that Marilyn was one of his street dealers, and her aunt was hanging on him. He used to ask her questions about the old man's business. So, Sandra and I took advantage of the chance to put the squeeze on Henderson. Sergei went along with it. He'd get one of his gofers to take the dough from whoever delivered it, and then he'd hand it over to me."

"Okay," I said, absorbing all this. "And Relgado just helped out of the goodness of his heart?"

"No. We'd owe him a favor—big time. That was the way he put it."

"I can't buy all that," I said. "There's got to be more to it than that."

"If it wasn't for the frame, I wouldn't be talking to you at all," Manfred said.

"So why don't you go to the police?"

"I've got a record. And the blackmail deal. They'll figure if I did the blackmail, I'd do the murders."

Well, that did make some sense. "The police can't see you killing Walker and then leaving your own gun behind. A gun registered in your own name. How did you get a gun license with your record anyway?"

"Henderson pulled some strings," Paul said.

"Figures. What about the killings?"

"I'm out that," he said. "I had nothing to do with it. Maybe it was Sergei."

"Maybe. And maybe not."

"Henderson told me to talk to you, and I have. Are you going to help me?"

"What do you want from me?"

"I don't know. I'm hot right now. Maybe you can take the 50 grand off my hands?"

I laughed. "I'm not that stupid. All you would have to do is tip off the cops that I have the money, and I'm on the hook for blackmail. Maybe the police will throw in a murder or two."

"You don't trust anyone either," Paul said in quiet realization.

"I'm just not that stupid. I'm skeptical. I'm a forensic accountant by heart. I never trust people who only give me half a story. You're in this mess up to your eyeballs. Maybe you didn't kill anybody, but you know who did. I shouldn't even be talking to you."

"Maybe I need an ace in the hole."

"You're not holding any cards. You want to go for a fall, that's your business."

He was sweating now, and he looked at me like he was getting desperate. "Maybe I have a crazy idea."

"Like what?"

"You're an honest guy, ain't you?"

I looked straight at him.

"I'm glad you didn't bring the cops," he said, and started to walk away.

"Who's behind it?" I called to him.

He heard me, and he kept on going. I stood up, and he walked under the arch and onto Fifth Avenue.

I sat back down on the bench and watched the drug dealers in action. They'd stroll up to a customer, reach into their own mouth and pull a rock of crack out from their cheek, haggle, and hand it over for $30, cash. Customer stashes the rock in his own mouth. Lost in the crowd. Great way to pass AIDS, I thought—never mind hepatitis. They carry it in their cheek because crack won't dissolve in saliva—and they can swallow the rock if police start questioning them. How did the buyer know he wasn't getting a chunk of wax with a little crack powder sprinkled on it? Guess he just found out later. *Caveat emptor*. It was getting chilly, and I felt hungry. May was just a couple of days away.

I didn't want to take time to eat. I just wanted to think. Manfred had been framed by someone who wanted him out of the way. He thought it was Sandra who had taken his gun, after she had helped him pull off the blackmail scheme. Did Sandra shoot Bram Walker? Did she shoot Teddy Noren?

How much truth was there in what Manfred told me? What kind of help did he think he was going to get from me, anyway? Why didn't I get some food after all, and give my mind a break?

I found a Mexican restaurant on University Place and ate a beef enchilada with chili and beans and slugged down a big lemonade.

I called Hildy and told her I was going home, and to tell Tom he could take off and do whatever he wanted.

The phone was ringing when I opened the door to my apartment. It was Myra. "Where have you been Lenny?" she said. "You don't work twenty-four hours a day, do you?" Her voice was smooth, musical.

"I'm training to become a social pariah."

"I can come over, and we can train together," She cooed.

"I'm world weary. A sunk cost. A write-off. Not fit company for anyone."

"How about lunch tomorrow?"

"I'll have to call you."

"Have you heard anything about Paul?"

"Not a thing," I evaded.

"There was nothing in the papers."

"You want the papers to print that the police are still looking for him? That's not what they call news anymore. When the police find him, there will be an item in the newspaper. If they prove he did the murders, then it will be a big story. Maybe it will make a headline story on cable TV."

"Do you think Paul killed Bram and Teddy?" Her voice was almost sultry. Weird.

"I'm too tired to think. I just want to crash in front of my TV and watch a good movie — maybe *The Quite Place* from Netflix."

"But it's so early."

"I'll call you tomorrow."

There was nothing worth watching on TV, so I poured myself a cold ginger ale, sat on my couch and vegged-out for an hour. I tried to keep the Hendersons and the Rileys out of my brain.

I went to the bookshelf and found Coleridge:

*In Xanadu did Kubla Khan*

*A stately pleasure-dome decree*

*Where Alph, the sacred river, ran*

*Through caverns measureless to man*

*Down to a sunless sea.*

I wasn't entirely a fool. Samuel Taylor Coleridge. Nineteenth century English lyrical poet. Young. Gifted. His prodigal career was cut short when he died of a drug overdose. *"There's nothing new under the sun,"* I reflected. Isn't that what Solomon said? Well there was nothing left to do but try to get some sleep and start again tomorrow morning.

I put away Coleridge and went to the bathroom where I boiled for half an hour in my wonderful Jacuzzi. Then went to bed. I took the phone off the hook. If anyone wanted me, they'd have to kick down the front door. Nobody kicked down my front door.

I was thankful for that. With my next stop the great state of Texas, at least I'd be temporarily away from the Hendersons.

My cell phone rang. "Hello Dad." It was my daughter, Rebecca "How are you doing?"

"Fine I hope," I replied.

"How about you?"

"Have a major managerial accounting exam tomorrow. Can you come down and take it for me?" She laughed. "Just kidding, but my roommate and I have a couple of questions."

"Fire away," I said. "I'm really glad you called. Have you switched to accounting yet?"

"No dad. Just taking a managerial accounting course so I'll know what you do for a living."

"You can find a job with an accounting degree," I replied sincerely.

"Okay, there are three cost estimation methods—high-low, work measurement, and the regression analysis methods. We know that regression analysis is more accurate but costlier. We know how to use algebra to determine an estimation line between representative high and low points in the data. The high or low data point corresponds to the high or low activity level—not the high or low-cost levels. Piece of cake."

"So, what is the problem?" I asked.

"We understand the work management approach generally involves a statistical method that measures the activity. Tell us about the regression approach."

"Regression analysis involves two types of variables. The dependent variable is the cost to be estimated. One or more independent variables can be used as the cost driver to estimate the amount of the dependent variable. Most of the time we try to use only one independent variable, the one that most closely drives the cost of the dependent variable."

"Okay," I continued. "You can use Excel to create a scatter plot of historical cost-volume data, look for outliers, and add the regression line, regression equation, and R-squared figure to the scatter plot. You then compare the high-low line with the regression line and choose between two potential cost drivers based upon the R-square of the regressions. Got it."

"We'll study some more," Rebecca replied.

We discussed several other topics before Rebecca hung up. I really appreciated her call, which cheered me up.

# Twelve

*Forensic accounting refers to the application of accounting principles, theories, and discipline to facts or hypotheses at issue in a legal dispute and encompasses every branch of accounting knowledge.*

— AICPA Management Advisory Services Technical Consulting Practice Aid
No. 7: *Litigation Services*

My flight to Fort Worth allowed me to continue my preparation for the courtroom battle the next day. Forensic accounting covers two broad areas: investigative accounting and litigation support. The AICPA describes litigation services as any professional assistance non-lawyers provide to lawyers in the litigation process. The Henderson case was allowing me to serve as an investigative accountant, although I felt like I was having to act more like a detective than an accountant. That was not my objective.

In violent crimes, there's usually little doubt a crime has been committed. You spend most of your time trying to prove who the criminal was. In a financial fraud, you may know who the perpetrator is. What you must do is demonstrate that the actions committed constituted fraud. Fraud is an intentional misrepresentation of a material fact, upon which there is reliance by a victim, who suffers consequential damages. The Henderson engagement had attributes of financial crime and violent crime, making it particularly difficult. It was Red collar crime rather than white collar crime. Forensic accountants and whistleblowers have sometimes been killed.

Rick Mannino had sent me two newspaper articles from the *Dallas Times Herald*. A reporter, Robert Deitz, described the stereotype image of an accountant, "After all, everyone knows that bean counters are bespectacled, pale skinned wretches who spend mind-numbing lives in dreary cubicles poring over faint computer printouts and dusty ledgers. Right?" But not the image of accountants in the movie *The Accountant*, of course.

Tomorrow I'd be testifying in court for General Dynamics as an expert witness and providing other litigation support. Working in concert with high-powered attorneys, and keeping a clear-headed, unemotional bearing under intensive cross examination was my job. I was to provide credible opinion on complex cost allocation issues. The opposing attorney's job would be trying to make me look like an absolute lying idiot. Any anger, loss of confidence, or other emotional lapse he or she can drive or insult me into, will work to their advantage. My experience as a professor would be in my favor, since I've made a career out of boiling down complex accounting issues into clear, understandable terms.

What I need to guard against most, is treating the jury like my students, getting too personally sensitive to attacks, and being too slow to catch leading questions before I fall for them. The opposing lawyer will accuse me of grandstanding and thinking I'm back in my ivory tower. During my previous deposition he tried to make me look like a fool. He substituted words and tried to get me to agree to ideas I'm not advocating—so my statements would show up later on written transcripts he can quote to show me contradicting myself. On my deposition I had done well. No major damage. The expert on the other side also had done well, so we were in the courtroom to solve the dispute.

I would soon be in the courtroom. The judge *owns* the courtroom, and basically referees the lawyers to keep them from abusing the evidence process. The witness is just a guest, providing one more form of evidence—evidence the other party will work overtime to impeach or contradict in any way they can.

But, I liked the work of preparing beforehand, and getting grilled and drilled for a courtroom battle over accounting principles. There was always the challenge to react and lash back at the many innuendoes and leading questions staged by the opposing attorney. You had to be a little bit of a glutton for punishment, and the stress was probably not worth the daily fees I was getting. But I enjoyed doing it. Sometimes I imagined the opposing attorney was like a black clad medieval knight, thundering toward me on horseback with a sharp lance. I always toppled the evil knight in my daydreams. But not always in court. You win some, you lose some, no matter how good you are.

Another Dallas newspaper article by John A. Bolt gave one reason for forensic accountants:

*Robbers do not need guns. Pencil and paper will do. Opportunity and greed are thievery's driving forces. Put enough zeroes behind a number, and it's amazing how flexible morals become. How many years in prison would you do to accumulate half a billion dollars in your bank account?*

They say white collar crime is the crime of choice—because the dollar amounts are enormous, and the probability of going to jail is slim. But, I know a guy who defrauded investors out of $200 million. When he went to jail, it was no federal country club. They put him in a high security prison for violent offenders. It cost him a couple of thousand dollars every month in payoffs to the gangs inside the prison, just to stay alive, and to get his laundry done.

I took a taxi to the Westin Hotel, in the Galleria, off LBJ Freeway at the Dallas Parkway. Inside my room, I picked up the Guest Informant. An article by A.D. Greene described Dallas from the air:

*The country under the jet's wing is green, not brown; the landscape is dotted with lakes large and small, so many they look like various-sized bits of broken mirror scattered about the landscape.*

I turned on the television and saw a David Letterman rerun list his top ten reasons for being an accountant. I caught a few.

- CPAs always have lead in their pencils.
- Old accountants never die, they just lose their balance.
- Accountants are calculating.
- Ticking comes naturally to accountants.
- Accountants: the few, the proud, the boss.

Later Bob Newhart, a former accountant, came on to promote his movie: Naked Gun 357. Reruns, I thought.

* * *

"Professor Cramer, for the court's record, please state your full name and current address."

"Paul Leonard Cramer, the third, 1250 Liberty Court, New York, New York."

"Dr. Cramer, we want to thank you for testifying today as an expert witness about certain accounting matters. First, I have several questions for you concerning your background. Where did you obtain you Ph.D. degree?"

"University of Illinois."

"Where did you receive your MBA degree?"

"Harvard University."

"Where did you receive your bachelor's degree?"

"Amherst."

"Are you listed in *Who's Who in America*?"

"Yes."

"What years were you president of the American Accounting Association?"

"That was 1996–97."

I'd rehearsed most of these questions and answers the night before. I was wearing my nice, dark blue suit that catches everything but money and women.

"Professor Cramer, have you written any accounting books?"

"I have written four accounting books. Two cost accounting textbooks, a forensic accounting book, plus an accounting casebook for MBA students."

"Would you please explain what is meant by forensic accounting?"

"Briefly, forensic accounting deals with the relation and application of accounting facts to business and social problems." I smiled and turned toward the jury. "As I tell my students, a forensic accountant is like the old TV Columbo or Quincy characters, except he or she uses accounting records and facts to uncover fraud, locate missing assets, document insider trading, calculate damages, and examine other white-collar crimes." I turned back to the pinstriped lawyer.

"Dr. Cramer, where are you currently employed?"

"I am the Sidney Paton Endowed Professorship of Accounting at Columbia University."

"Is it an honor to hold a named Endowed Professorship?"

"Yes, there are relatively few professorships in accounting." I thought, yes, but no money, just a title. The real money is in the 'chair' designations. I was still searching for an endowed chair at a major university.

"Professor Cramer, are you a Certified Public Accountant?"

"Yes, I've been licensed in New York, since 1985," I responded.

"Are you a member of the American Institute of CPAs?"

"Yes, since 1985."

"Do you serve on the Board of Directors of any major corporations?"

"Yes, I serve on the Board of Directors for four of the top Fortune one hundred companies, and for three smaller companies."

"Dr. Cramer, are you an outside consultant?"

"Yes."

"Please estimate how many professional articles you have written."

"About 120." I shifted in the wooden chair.

"Uh," the attorney shuffled several pages and then continued, "Have you ever appeared as an expert witness in court before?"

"Yes. I have been an expert witness for accounting matters on 11 different occasions—two oil companies, two banks, one insurance company, a manufacturing company, an accounting firm, the Internal Revenue Service, the SEC, and two divorce cases."

The attorney turned to the judge and said, "Your Honor, we present to this court Dr. Cramer, as an expert witness in the area of forensic cost accounting."

The robed judge turned to the opposing attorney and said, "Mr. Fletcher, do you have any objections to this request?"

Attorney Fletcher stood up and spoke plainly, "No, your Honor."

"So moved. You may proceed, counselor."

The other side had not used a *Daubert* challenge to try to stop me from being an expert witness. In district courts and many state courts an expert must survive *Daubert* challenges to their credentials. Today, judges determine whether to allow an expert to testify in a dispute. They are the gatekeepers.

"Dr. Cramer, what type of cost is the security service with General Dynamics? The approximately $16 million expense for security guards, cameras, alarms, and other expenditures."

"These costs would be classified as indirect costs. According to the Federal Acquisition Regulations, an indirect cost is one not directly identified with a single, final cost objective. It is identified with two or more final cost objectives, or an intermediate cost objective."

"Professor, what should be done with these indirect costs?" the attorney for General Dynamics asked, anticipating my rehearsed answer.

"These indirect costs, such as the security expenses, should be accumulated by logical cost groupings, with due consideration of the reason for incurring the expenditures. Since these indirect overhead costs are common to more than one department, they should be shared. Each department should be charged with its fair share of these security costs."

"Now Professor Cramer, how are these costs shared with the various departments?"

"Obviously these costs must be allocated to the various departments with a reasonable allocation base. This allocation base must be fair and equitable.

Think of it as a cost driver—an activity or procedure that causes the costs to be incurred."

"What would be a good cost driver for these security costs, Dr. Cramer?" The attorney smiled slightly.

I shifted in the hard seat and then replied, facing the jury. Always face the jury. "These costs are general and administrative expenses. Like personnel costs. They could be allocated based on either number of employees, labor hours, or labor costs."

"And who should determine how costs should be allocated: the government or the contractor?"

"Cost allocation should be the function of the contractor, not the government. The selection of an accounting system is the responsibility and prerogative of management—as long as the procedure follows generally accepted accounting principles and Cost Accounting Standards Board principles."

"How does General Dynamics allocate these costs?"

"By total direct engineering labor hours."

"Does this allocation method meet the generally accepted accounting practices you described?"

"Yes, it does," I replied with conviction.

* * *

The attorneys each act in the role of opposing movie directors—calling witnesses and orchestrating carefully timed presentations. All of it is designed to sway the jury's opinion in favor of their respective client's position. Civil cases, like this one, are decided based only on which side has the greater weight of evidence in its favor. Fifty-one percent of the evidence in your favor is theoretically all you need to win in a civil case. On the other hand, evidence of guilt or innocence beyond a reasonable doubt is the criterion for deciding criminal cases. It's a tougher standard and didn't apply to this case. As it turned out my role was relatively small in this one, but the *per diem* fees I received were decent.

Attorney Fletcher stood up. "Dr. Cramer, please tell the court how many years you have worked as an accountant in the defense industry."

"I have worked as an accountant in other industries, but not for a defense contractor." Here it comes, I thought.

"You have never worked for a defense contractor? Well then, can you tell the court please, how many years you have worked as the Chief Financial Officer of a major industrial corporation like General Dynamics?"

"I've had several responsible positions in accounting, but I have not worked as a Chief Financial Officer."

"Never been a Chief Financial Officer?" He paused. "Well, perhaps you can tell us Dr. Cramer, if you've ever taught a course on accounting for aerospace companies."

"Universities offer few courses on specific industries …"

"With all due respect, Dr. Cramer," he cut me off. "Have you ever taught a course on accounting for aerospace companies?"

"No, but …"

"Then you have formed your opinions in this dispute on just what you've been told, haven't you?"

"I have experience with large industrial companies and the principles …"

"Dr. Cramer," he cut me off again. "Isn't it true that you have published several professional articles critical of federal cost accounting standards, and you have a personal stake in the legal outcome of this case?"

"Objection Your Honor." Thankfully my attorney spoke before I could answer. "Two-part question."

"Sustained."

"Your Honor allow me to rephrase my question." Fletcher had already achieved his innuendo. "Dr. Cramer, because of the nature of your research, you have a personal stake in the outcome of this case, don't you."

"No." I knew where he was headed.

"No? Haven't you made your career by criticizing federal cost accounting standards in your writings?"

"No, I have not."

Fletcher "accidentally" dropped the sheaf of papers he was holding. While he was picking them up, he asked, "With all due respect, Doctor, haven't you published several articles critical of the Cost Accounting Standards Board?"

"Not that I recall." A hundred twenty articles I've published over the years. Some were critical reviews. Were any derogatory of the CASB? I couldn't think of any—except maybe my surrealistic accounting dream a few nights ago.

Attorney Fletcher muttered to himself, shuffling through the papers as he reorganized them. "Ah, there they are," he said, as if to himself. Looking over his glasses at me, then looking back at his papers, then back at me. "*Never* wrote any articles criticizing the CASB?" He sniffed. Shook his head in disapproval and obvious disbelief, turned his back to me.

The jury looked like they were buying it. This part always got under my skin. Don't let him get to you Lenny, I reminded myself. He's only doing his job.

"Think carefully now, Dr. Cramer. The taxpayers of this country stand to overpay tens of millions of hard earned dollars to this contractor. Isn't it true that you have no experience in the aerospace industry, and you were hired because of your professional bias on these cost accounting issues?"

"No … Well, I haven't been a CFO of …" Darn, always give the explanation *first*, the answer *second*. I hated when I slipped up on the spot like that.

"Haven't been a CFO! Never worked in the industry! Never taught a course on the subject! Don't even 'recall' the subject of the published articles you've built your academic career on?"

"I've …" He cut me off again.

"Your Honor, I have no further questions for this witness."

"You may step down, Dr. Cramer."

Well, he got me off the stand, and he cut at my credibility. Shot two birds with one stone. Did the jury buy it? I've seen partners from Big-4 CPA firms walk off the witness stand, head for the men's room and literally cry after some of these grillings. You can't lose your perspective. They're just doing their job—and earning their fees. This attorney wasn't too bad. Sometimes they slash you to ribbons and leave you feeling like you're lying on the floor bleeding to death. Having the hide of a rhinoceros doesn't hurt in this business.

When my court appearance was over, I had some time before my flight back to New York. So, I walked from my room in the Westin to the Galleria lobby. Several people were walking around with COPAS nametags: Council of Petroleum Accountants Societies. There was a seminar in the hotel for oil and gas accounting instructors, sponsored by COPAS and the University of North Texas.

As I started walking into the Galleria, I passed a Gallery of History store. Inside I saw a 1948 baseball signed by Jackie Robinson—$19,995. There was a red boxing glove signed by Muhammad Ali, $4,199.

A lot of the historic items were business related. Lottery ticket number 120 was signed by George Washington in 1768: $22,240. The display said that in Colonial times, lotteries were a popular way to raise funds for roads in Virginia, Maryland, and Pennsylvania. So, we still think we can gamble our way out of government deficits? I shook my head.

A canceled check for $22.04 signed in 1928 by Thomas A. Edison, $2,100. A Rick Nelson check for $1,307 signed in 1985, $5,312. A $28.05 canceled check signed by Orville Wright in 1945, $1,955. Amazing.

"Hello, may I help you? I'm Tim Proudfoot."

"I bet a lot of people ask you if you're an Indian," I said.

"Yeah. Actually, I'm Irish."

After talking with Tim for some time, he told me that in college he had a full-blooded Indian friend named Riley. They had a lot fun with the two names.

"We bring history alive," was Tim's description of the gallery.

I continued to walk around the gallery. Saw a manuscript signed by George Washington in 1798 selling for $63,000. Astronaut Neil Armstrong signature on poem with photograph, $29,597, and signed picture of Gene Cernan — the last astronaut to walk on the moon, and the only man to walk on the moon twice, $1,826. A signed photo of Adolf Hitler, $64,850.

They even had a Geronimo photograph. His signature was printed in big letters — not signed. $35,000. The Human Tiger was called the greatest General that ever lived by U.S. Senator Foraker. Abraham Lincoln photo, proclamation, and signature, $25,500.

I almost bought a baseball signed by the eight living pitchers who pitched a perfect game. My favorite Dodger, Sandy Koufax, was one of them. Instead, I bought a book.

In the center of the Galleria was an ice skating rink. Mostly kids with white, green, orange, or black skates went around and around in circles. There were three cascading chandeliers rising to the glass ceiling. They were about three stories tall.

There were real trees around the rink, and in the food court. After an enchilada at the El Fenix Café, I took a taxi to the play *Beauty and the Beast*. Belle, the beauty, is dissatisfied with her life in a small provincial French town. An avid reader, she is constantly trying to fend off misplaced affections of a conceited Gaston.

Her father Maurice, an inventor, gets lost in the woods and is imprisoned by the Beast. The Beast is really an enchanted prince, who had a spell put on him by an enchanter because he had no love in his arrogant heart for others.

Belle offers herself instead of her father, and the Beast accepts her as a replacement. Under the spell the Beast had to give love and receive love to become a prince again. Belle does find the prince inside the Beast. Of course, there was a happy ending to the fairy tale.

During the play I determined that Henderson was a combination of Gaston and the Beast.

On the way to the airport the next morning, I saw a bumper sticker on a Mercedes as we left the parking lot. "I ❤ MY CPA." I needed to get one of those.

On my flight back to New York, I read my new book, *Collecting Historical Documents: A Guide to Owning History*, by Todd M. Axelrod. One autograph letter, dated August 13, 1941, signed by "Old Blood and Guts" George S. Patton, Jr. caught my attention. In a letter to the headmaster at his son's school, Patton said about his son, "George is a poor student — possibly stupid." The kid probably grew up with a lot of confidence.

I picked up the *Wall Street Journal* — Southwest edition. The Hazirian Liberation Army had exploded a bomb, in a small spur off a midtown New York subway tunnel. They wanted to show us their capability. The spur collapsed, and a dozen people were critically injured. Thankfully nobody was killed. Forensic demolition experts were trying to recover pieces of the bomb for analysis. The Hazirians said we had just 72 hours left to meet their demands, before they blew up the Social Security Administration buildings.

A Section B article on the prices at a recent Sotheby's art auction caught my attention. Among other items, it listed the sale of a three-dimensional painting in folded lead by Jannis Kounellis. Kounellis … Kounellis … I hurriedly opened my briefcase and pulled out the list of paintings sold by Myra's art gallery. There it was. Sold in the same month. But a month is a long time.

When I returned home, Rebecca had left a message on my phone at home that she had made 93 on her managerial accounting examination. A good kid.

# Thirteen

*Get this in your head. There is only one indicator for telling the value of paintings, and that is in the salesroom.*

—Renoir

The next morning, I showed Hildy the *Wall Street Journal* article I'd read on the plane from Dallas. I asked her to contact Sotheby's and see if they'd fax us any information they had on the Kounellis painting's provenance: dates, prices, history of previous ownership—anything they had.

I skipped breakfast, and Hildy sent out for coffee and Danish. Tom wasn't here, and I sent for him. When the coffee arrived, he helped himself to some of it.

I told him about my little meeting with Paul Manfred before leaving for Texas.

"You should have grabbed him," Tom said.

"Where would that get me? He'd just clam up."

"At least now you know who masterminded the great blackmail racket."

"Yeah. Fifty thousand dollars. But Sandra has a lot more to lose if she gets caught."

"And don't forget our pal Sergei," Tom said. He was perched on the edge of my desk. "So now Paul owes him. He's going to collect on that one. That's for sure."

"Maybe Relgado's got something bigger in mind. Why would he go along with the two of them, unless he was going to gain heavy leverage—maybe force one of them to take a fall for him on something," I speculated.

145

"Aah. We're nowhere again."

"Paul didn't look too worried for a guy who has an army of police after him, either."

"And he asked something about an 'ace in the hole'?" Tom said as he squeezed his forehead, "I think Manfred gave you a line about just wanting fifty grand."

"Maybe so."

"You think Henderson will help him with this murder charge?"

"Paul doesn't think so," I informed Tom. "He seems somewhat bitter about Henderson."

"Could be an act."

"Listen, I can't go around testing everybody with a lie detector. It would be great if everyone told me the truth. But some people are occupational liars."

Yes, and some are pathological liars, I thought.

"Now for the good news," I announced. "I found some evidence that at least one of the paintings sold at Myra's gallery had to be a fake." I told Tom about the sale of the Greek Jannis Kounellis painting at a Sotheby's auction, and that it was one of the paintings on the gallery's sales list he had given me.

Hildy poked her head in the office. "There's a Frank Masters here to see you."

I told Tom to duck out and check the local buyer of the Jannis Kounellis painting from Myra's gallery—to see if the buyer was a fake too.

Hildy showed Masters to my office. He was dressed in a navy-blue blazer, beige pants, and penny loafers. No pennies in the loafers. As he sat down, he looked nervous, and his hands were trembling. It didn't look like an act. He was scared all right.

"I've been threatened," the artist said.

"By who?"

"I—I don't know."

He saw my skeptical look, and he wrung his hands even more. "What difference does it make? I can't go to the police. I don't know what to do."

"You can't go to the police because it has to do with your drug dealing?" I said.

"There's no use now, is there?"

"I'm an accountant. Why did you come to me?"

"I need help. I'm willing to pay."

"I'm no bodyguard. I try to avoid criminal expert witnessing. You make your bed, and then you lie in it."

"Look, I didn't expect *this*. That's the truth. Look, we needed the money ... drug dealing was one thing, but people are getting *murdered*. I knew there were risks, but—" He started to chew his lip.

"Sergei Relgado is bad company."

"Drugs are just a side show for him," Masters said.

"I guess you'd know about as much as I do."

"Yeah. Well, he's got his hands in all kinds of things. Then Teddy gets blown away, then Bram. And I'm next. And—"

"And what?"

"Princess came to see me. She works for Sergei. She recruits the girls off the street to deal for us. She told me it would be better for everyone if I just took off and didn't come back. She said she was warning me as a favor to Nadja. I haven't even seen Nadja for a couple of days. The Princess looked at me like I was dead already. Then later when I went across the street to get breakfast, a car came screeching around the corner and almost hit me. I didn't know where else I could go. You have to help me."

"Who took the scales out of Teddy's apartment?" I asked.

"Bram did."

"Who killed Teddy?"

"I don't know. Look, I don't. It couldn't have been Bram. He wouldn't kill anyone. And I didn't do it."

"Something has been puzzling me," I said. "I found a canvas in Teddy Noren's apartment. An oil painting. Teddy only used acrylics. Why would the killer blow Noren away, then sit around painting a picture?"

"That painting has nothing to do with Teddy's death," Masters said.

"How do you know?"

"Look, Teddy painted the picture in acrylic. I went over it with oil."

Answers. What a delight.

"Some of us do it that way. We do a painting in acrylic, then we go over it with oil. We did that lots of times. I was with Teddy in his apartment the day he got killed. I had my oils with me. We'd been working on the painting for weeks. He put the canvas up and asked me to go over some parts of it with my oils. That's all. Then I left. When I found out that Teddy was dead, I didn't want anyone to find out I'd been there that day. So, I kept my mouth shut. You can have an expert check the canvas. Under the oil you'll find acrylic."

"Why didn't Teddy just do it himself?"

"He didn't like working with oils. It wasn't his medium. What difference does it make?"

"None, I guess, except it was a forgery of Giovanni Bellini's *Madonna*. Why?"

"Hey, I just put oil over the acrylic. Copying the masters is good for you."

So, the acrylic was an intermediate product that is transferred during the manufacturing process from one subunit to another subunit of an organization. The intermediate product may be further worked on by the receiving subunit or sold to an external customer. Noren's acrylic paintings could be sold as he had completed them, or Masters could have touched them up with oil colors and sold them at a potentially higher price—especially if they were good forgeries. Life really does imitate cost accounting. If only my students could realize this fact on their annoying student evaluation of teaching forms. This dysfunctional internal control feature has destroyed higher education because of grade inflation and coursework deflation. A's are as common as dirt at most universities, especially the private ones.

Similarly, when managers use budgets to align with the goals of an organization, this alignment of managerial and organizational goals is called goal congruence. However, when a budget is improperly administered, managers may subvert the organization's goals by using money for purposes other than for the best interest of the organization. This dysfunctional behavior occurs in business organizations just like the current dysfunctional performance measurement of professors throughout the U.S. Or, in manufacturing, the manager can decide to increase production so as to spread fixed production costs over the additional units produced and held in inventory. The firm's precious "cash" is now tied up in its inventment in work in progress and finished goods inventories.

I actually believed Masters with respect to painting oil over the acrylic. It was easy enough to check it out by having someone take a closer look at the painting. But why bother at this point? His story made sense. And he knew it could be checked out easily enough. Maybe he never even knew that Teddy and Marilyn were probably using the paintings to cover up the drug proceeds for Sergei Relgado. Money laundering. Hard even for the IRS to catch. But did that get him off the hook? He could still have killed Noren before he left that day. But why?

Art and antiques are an excellent way to launder illegal money. A person can sell the fake artwork at full value to the drug operator. Bingo, they have cleaned the money and avoided the anti-money laundering laws. Banks must file a report if someone deposits cash transactions of $10,000 or more into the banks. The same for money transmitters such as Western Union. Western Union has an automated system to monitor all transactions that takes about 31 seconds. Otherwise, they would need 100,000 more analysts. However, in early 2018, Western Union had to forfeit $586 million for failure to maintain an effective anti-money laundering program and abetting wire fraud for three locations in New York.

Also, financial institutions must file suspicious activity reports. That is how they caught Eliot Spitzer, the then governor of New York state, patronizing a high-priced prostitution service. His bank reported suspicious money transfers.

"Look, you have to help me?" Masters pleaded.

"Best thing for you to do is to go the police," I said.

"Yeah, go to jail and be accused of murder."

"They might actually believe you." I doubted it, but they might.

Masters got up and walked to the window and looked out at the Chrysler Building.

"It looks like Relgado is cleaning out this operation," I said to his back. "I don't know why, but you probably know too much. If you want to live, you better get out of here—fast."

Masters turned to me. "Do you think Sergei killed Teddy and Bram?"

"It isn't exactly his style—shooting someone and leaving the gun behind to make it look like suicide."

"Teddy didn't have an enemy in the world," Masters said. "There were some people who didn't like Bram, but not bad enough to kill him."

"I haven't any answers."

Masters rubbed the knuckles of his right fist against his teeth. "I can't just leave everything behind. I have a life." He was agitated, torn.

Everything had mushroomed into a deadly nightmare for him. He couldn't out run an organized criminal operation. If he went to the police, he might end up in jail. Maybe tried for a murder he didn't commit. Better that than dead.

Then he nodded at me slowly, and he moved toward the door and went out. I watched him go. One more lost soul.

The city was full of lost souls. It's New York City after all.

* * *

Sweet little Marilyn. I hadn't seen Marilyn in a while. I wondered what she was doing.

A little later Myra called me.

How about lunch?

Sure. Why not?

We can meet in Herald Square, in the small park, and decide where to go.

I told Hildy I was going out and would be back in a couple of hours.

Myra Riley was dressed in a white, knit suit. She looked out of place in the small park. There was the usual traffic jam in front of Macy's. I sat down on the bench beside her, and she took my hand and gave it a squeeze. "Well I hope you're not avoiding me, Lenny" she cooed.

"I've been busy. Had to go to Fort Worth. Trying to put the puzzle pieces together. Too many missing pieces, Myra."

"When the police catch Paul ..."

"You think that will solve everything?" I asked. "Don't be naive. Paul is just one small piece in this deadly puzzle."

She looked at a loss, and I didn't bother to explain any further. She could have been acting, or she knew something. Or maybe she knew everything, and I'd just be wasting my time. I didn't know much, but something was afoot, as my great uncle Sherlock Holmes used to say.

We found an English steak house and had sliced beef on rye. I drank a Dr. Pepper, remembering the sign in the Ballpark in Arlington. "Have you seen Marilyn lately?" I asked.

"Yesterday."

"What's she doing?"

"Nothing now."

The gravy was peppery. I ran a piece of beef around in it and savored the flavor.

"Did you want to talk to Marilyn?" she asked.

"Where would that get me?"

"You think Marilyn is evading you?"

"As much as anyone else in this situation." I watched her drink and wondered just how innocent she really was. I didn't think she killed the two artists. I was reasonably sure Relgado didn't. But Relgado could've had one of his thugs try to run down Masters—if he really was clearing out his drug operation for some reason. Maybe he feared some heat, or it was something bigger. I had the feeling it had to be something bigger.

"Did your father ever talk to you about his new microchip? Some high-speed sub-miniature thing? Anything about which competitors it might hurt? Anything like that?"

"Are you kidding? We don't talk much. We don't even see each other much. And when I was living at the house, he never talked to me about his business plans."

"He doesn't have anything valuable in his house, or in some vault does he—like artifacts or jewelry?"

"No. He doesn't collect anything but his paintings."

"Now who mentioned paintings to me? Sandra, wasn't it? Yeah. Sandra."

"The prize, of course, is the Turner."

"The English painter?"

"Yes. But he keeps it locked up in a special room. You need a security code and a special key to get past all his alarms."

"Turner? Maybe that's the McGuffey that Sandra mentioned to me."

"The thing everybody wants. Like in the Hitchcock movies," she said.

"That's right," I said guardedly. "In a secure room?"

"There's Picasso, Braque ..."

"Are they real? Any forgeries?" I was amazed.

She appeared shocked. "He only buys originals."

"Let's get out of here," I said.

West 57th Street was loaded with art galleries. Not the schlock chain store galleries. These were the real thing. If you had the data, that is. Henri Matisse, John Singer Sargent, Winslow Homer, Klimt, and Kokoschka. We stopped at the first gallery. The sales clerk was prissy and probably wondered if we'd lost our way. When Myra described the Turner, his face glowed like he was plugged into a nuclear reactor.

While the clerk gushed with his face, I was admiring a Remington. I'd discovered that Texas sunsets really do look like that. "How much would that Joseph Turner be worth today?" I asked the clerk when Myra had finished.

"Well, one sold about two years ago for three million," the clerk said. "My name is Alexander Peers." He handed me a business card. "Turner was renowned for his oil paintings. He is known as the 'painter of light.'"

"I imagine it would have to be sold in an auction in order to get the best price, wouldn't it?" I asked.

"Oh, of course."

"What about a stolen one?"

"Stolen?" He was indignant. "No reputable dealer would touch it. Maybe some unscrupulous private collector—but they could never put it on display. Why do you ask?"

"But there are collectors who do that, aren't there?"

"Unfortunately, yes," the clerk sighed. "Artwork, stamps, coins. One stolen Brasher Doubloon worth half million dollars has never turned up. In the hands of a dishonest private collector, I suppose."

"What would the price be for a hot Turner?"

"That's difficult to say. There are so many factors in that type of a situation. A Turner. Three million, I would guess. Possibly four. In 2006, Christie's New York auctioned Giudecca, *La Donna Della Salute and Sam Giorgio*, a view of Venice exhibited at the Royal Academy in 1841 for $35.8 million, possibly to casino magnate Stephen Wynn."

"You know the art market experienced a retreat in the late eighties. Prices for some impressionists declined as much as 50 percent from the peak in 1989. But the market recovered in '92, and now is definitely the time to buy. Why recently Nympheas de fleur by Claude Monet sold for $84.7 million dollars."

I resisted the sales pitch. "And if a Turner turned up in an auction today?"

"Oh, much more now. Few Turners come up for auction you know. The museums never give them up. The private collectors who own them would never sell, unless they were experiencing financial, uh ... embarrassment."

I took Myra's hand, thanked the clerk, and we left. Her hand felt soft.

"You must be wrong," Myra said outside, on the sidewalk, with a warm sun overhead. "No one can get anywhere near that Turner. It would be like breaking into a bank vault."

"Vaults have been broken into before."

"But who?"

"Cora. Sandra."

"Not Cora. She's very content with what she has, believe me. And Sandra—well, she has what she wants."

"You sure about that?"

"She won't go against my father. That would be dumb—she'd get cut out of his will. She wouldn't dare antagonize him."

"For two or three million dollars, I think she might take a chance. Then she'd really be independent. I wonder if the Turner is what your father donated to Columbia University."

"What are you talking about."

"Oh, that's the reason I'm involved in this whole engagement. Your father donated some of his appreciated art collection to Columbia University. My president asked me—uh, twisted my arm—to help him out with this family 'financial problem.'"

"Oh, I don't think he'd have given the Turner away," she concluded.

I said almost to myself, "In a charitable remainder trust, the donor irrevocably gives up the asset. They take a tax deduction based upon the age of the donor and get income for life."

"Why would my father need income for life?"

"I don't know. Maybe he has a cash flow problem we don't know about. Even billionaire Catwoman Jocelyn Wildenstein had to file for bankruptcy recently, showing a Citibank balance of zero. But for someone with highly appreciated assets, a charitable remainder trust is a great way to improve cash flow and make a charitable gift at the same time. But you do give up the asset—in this case, the paintings he donated."

We started walking toward Fifth Avenue. "If Sandra did try to get her hands on the Turner," Myra said, "how would she ever get rid of it? She would need a private collector—someone willing to buy it who didn't care if they ever displayed the painting or not—someone who would buy stolen art."

"Who meets all kinds of art collectors? Artists."

"And art galleries," she added.

I gently asked her about her sale of the three-dimensional lead painting by Jannis Kounellis. As best she could remember, Marilyn had sold the painting to a customer for about $180,000. I didn't press the issue further.

We had a pleasant walk in the park, and then we had dinner. I put her in a cab. She gave me a warm smile. Her eyes looked delicate. They floated up into mine unguarded. I felt myself lean forward. I touched her hair, and then her temple. I caressed my thumb across her cheek, back to her ear, I put my hand gently under her head. Lifting it toward me, I kissed her lips. She responded with a sensitivity that was electrifying. I smiled, shut the door, and walked to Park Avenue. It had been a long time since I'd remembered touching anyone like that.

I called the office on my cell phone. Hildy told me not much was happening. Sotheby's had agreed to fax or email us a copy of their auction prospectus, along with some other information, and she was waiting on its arrival. I shut my cell phone and took a bus to 42nd Street, got an add-a-ride, took the cross-town, and went to the office.

Tom was there, and I brought him to my office and told him what I thought. He told me what he had found when he verified some of the art sales at Myra's gallery.

"Fake paintings are being used to launder drug money," he said. "Could be we're starting to make some progress. I looked for the customer who bought the Kounellis painting—phony all right. The address was an abandoned warehouse in Brooklyn. Not as exotic as chasing a brilliant red ruby through the Orient Express. Like something they call the Star of Asia."

"You can't have everything."

"We just don't live right, Lenny," he said. "A stolen ruby, a chase through a moving train, corpses in every compartment—that's the life for a Sherlock Holmes. What do we get? Gangster hits and money laundering."

"Gangster hits? You find out anything on the murders?"

"That is the only thing it can be. I've been thinking, and I just can't see anything else. Relgado ordered the hits. Had it set up to look like suicides, so the police won't even think of him."

It did make some sense the way Tom put it, but I just couldn't buy the whole theory. "And the motive?" I said.

"Maybe Sergei's a member of the Kill an Artist a Month Club," Tom speculated.

"So, you don't have a motive, do you?" I chided.

"How about cleaning up the operation. Maybe he's tired of dealing drugs."

"He kills two artists that are over their heads and know too much, who also paint fake masterpieces. But his recruiter warns the third one." I told Tom about Frank Masters and the attempt to run him down outside his apartment.

"Well, you can't say things aren't coming to a head."

"Try to track down some more of Myra's customers—who bought paintings sold by Marilyn. One bad customer address isn't enough evidence. We are in the evidence business, sir! I'm going to visit Marilyn."

Marilyn Riley was home, polishing her toe nails. She had on shorts and a gray sweatshirt with "Calvin Klein" across the front, with one foot on a hassock. Dark brown nail polish.

"What now?" she almost shouted.

"Did Teddy know many art collectors?"

"Of course. Who do you think bought his paintings, taxi drivers?"

"Did he know any rich art collectors? Like the kind that go for Picasso or Winslow?"

"If he did, we wouldn't have needed money. They wouldn't bother with someone like us. They wouldn't even go to the exhibits at the Village or on 59th Street. They all go to 57th Street. The kind of places where my grandfather goes."

"What about Bram and Frank?"

"I doubt it."

I watched her dab at a toenail with a little brush. "Have you heard from the Princess or Nadja?"

"You know about the Princess, huh? No, I haven't heard from either one of them in a couple of days."

My cell phone rang, and it was Hildy. "Excuse me," I said. "I am expecting Henderson to call."

Hildy said, "Mr. Henderson just called. He's in his office, and he wants you to call him ASAP."

And I did. "Where are you?" Henderson said.

I told him. He wanted the address, and I gave it to him.

"You wait for me outside. I'll pick you up in a few minutes. We'll go straight to my home."

"What's up?"

"Someone broke into my house." He sounded as if he was announcing a stock quotation. "One of my paintings was stolen. My pride and joy."

"The Turner?"

"How did you know?"

"That's obvious. It was your favorite."

Click.

The black Fleetwood limo sped away from SoHo. I sat in the back with Lloyd Henderson. "Sandra called me a half hour ago. She was incoherent as usual. She and the household staff were tied up and gagged. The thieves broke into the room where I keep my most valuable paintings. The alarms went off. But they worked incredibly fast. They took my Turner before the police got there. The police untied everyone, and Sandra called me. And I called you. I'm impressed with the way it was done, but that was my Turner, Dr. Cramer. I intend to get it back." He was furious.

"Where was Cora all this time?"

"She was tied up with the others. Humph. Sometimes I forget she's even there."

"I'm sure she appreciates that."

"Unfortunately, Cora is like an inanimate object. You see her, but she responds to nothing."

"She moves, breathes, and has feelings. Just like all the rest of us."

"Don't concern yourself with Cora, Doctor. When I die she'll be a rich woman. I doubt she'll travel or enjoy life. She's like part of my house. She won't leave it. She is conditioned. She is like one of the roses in my garden."

So much for fatherhood. We were going straight through by car. And we broke a few speed records while we were at it. Surprisingly, on the Long Island Expressway we didn't get stopped. Henderson was in a hurry to survey the damage. If he was seething inside, he was doing a good job of controlling it.

What makes the Hendersons of the world? Profit motive? Greed, I guess. Stone cold greed. The conscience is a funny thing. Some people feel guilty over borrowing a paper clip. For others, it's silent in the face of massive atrocities.

Henderson loved things, and he used people—even his own family members, and now he was getting the short end of the stick. There was silence in the car now, heavy. Henderson's face was dark, rigid. A professional gang had pulled off the robbery. Primed and timed. That meant only one thing to me—Sergei Relgado.

I thought I now knew why the artists had been killed. It had to all connect.

The place was swarming with Long Beach police. In the big front room, the household staff were being questioned by detectives, and fingerprint men were everywhere. I followed Henderson into the special room where his paintings were hanging on walls. There was a fortune here. Why didn't the thieves take everything? They took only his pride and joy.

One empty frame. The canvas had been taken from the frame and evidently rolled up. The Turner. Just rolled up and taken away.

A detective joined us. His name was Cyrus Balaban, first grade. He was tall and lanky, his face was angular, and he wore a plain gray suit and deadpan expression. From what he could gather from Cora, Sandra, and the servants, there'd been four or five people involved in the theft. They had all worn stockings over their heads. No one heard a car drive up. But after they'd been bound and gagged, and the painting taken, they'd all heard at least two cars pull away. There might have been a third car. No wonder Balaban was grim. So far, all the fingerprints found were from the employees and the sisters. But they couldn't account for one set, and they wanted to take Henderson's prints for comparison. He obliged, and he walked away with Balaban.

I moved from painting to painting, knowing I'd probably never see so many masterpieces in one room again. A Henri Matisse. An early Picasso. I came across three German expressionists, Erich Heckel, Ernst Ludwig Kirchner, and August Macke. The Macke showed a woman admiring a parrot in a shop window.

"Quite a collection, isn't it?" a subdued, feminine voice said.

She must walk like a cat, I thought as I turned around. There was a slight resemblance to Sandra, as I faced Cora Henderson. She wore a simple dress with puffed sleeves. "You know anything about art?" I asked.

"Something. Not much. I know my father loves these paintings. More than …"

"More than his daughters?" I said.

"I'm afraid so," she said hesitating, her face stiffened.

"These guys must have worked extremely fast."

"Yes. They were like lightning." Her meticulously shaped eyebrows lifted slightly.

"Don't you need a special key and security codes to get into this room?"

"Yes. They set off the alarm, but they must have gotten a key somehow. They didn't break through the door."

"Where did your father usually keep his key?"

"In his study, I believe. We never really knew."

"Easy enough for someone to borrow the key, make an impression, put it back, then have a copy made from the impression."

"I'm afraid I don't know anything about such matters Dr. Cramer," she said, and left the room. I was left alone with paintings I would never own myself and only see in museums. Paintings that some collectors would almost give their souls to own. Not a good deal.

I knew a coin collector once, who owned hundreds of rare coins. He valued them all, but he really treasured one more than all the others put together. It wasn't the most expensive one either. A Romanian pattern. Hadn't even cost him much.

The Joseph M. W. Turner painting was the prize in Henderson's collection, and I imagined it was probably because it was the most expensive — there wasn't much sentiment in Henderson.

Turner was a controversial, English Romantic painter known for his expressive colorization, imaginative landscapes, and often violent marine life paintings. Was the Turner stolen because it was the most valuable on the black market, or because it meant more to Henderson than the others? A psychological vendetta?

I wandered absently out to the back porch, sat down, and watched a dreary looking moon. Someone came up on the porch and stood quietly beside me for a moment. It was Sandra. I could smell her perfume. I liked the smell.

"Another detective is coming out from Manhattan," she stated. "A specialist in stolen art. Everybody wants to get in on the act."

"There's already too many people in this act," I said. Some fog rolled in from the Sound, as hazy as gauze, leaving the skin on my face feeling wet.

"Your mind must be working overtime," Sandra said.

"It's about time."

"So, you think you have it figured out?" Her voice sounded almost taunting.

"Some missing pieces. Everything will fall into place eventually. King Lear and his three daughters."

"Goneril, Cordelia, and Regan?" she coyed.

"How 'bout Cora, Sandra, and Myra," I said.

How did a stolen, genuine masterpiece fit with the money laundering scheme using fakes? My mind wrestled. The fog was heavier now, and I could hardly see her. Then I didn't see her. She'd retreated into the house. And I was alone in the fog.

For some reason downsizing came into my brain. It's an integral approach of configuring processes, products, and people to match costs to the activities that must be performed to operate efficiently and effectively in the present or future. If it doesn't add value, it is eliminated. Maybe it was right-sizing. How would Charles T. Horngren solve this problem?

I kept sitting. The U.S. dumping law popped into my vacant mind. Dumping occurs when a non-U.S. company sells a product in the U.S. at a price below the market value in the country where it's produced. Would the thieves dump the Turner at a discount? I needed to be writing an article, rather than chasing an art thief. Oh well, chasing a thief paid more money. At least I got more exercise. But would I survive academic life? I needed an article in *Accounting Review* or the *Journal of Accounting Research*.

# Fourteen

*In summary, each cost center needs:*
* *A clear definition of its boundaries,*
* *An estimate of the time period to accomplish measurable units of output, and*
* *An understanding of the cost drivers that explain variation in costs (if any) with variation in the activity level in the cost center.*

—H. Thomas Johnson and Robert S. Kaplan

He was a New York City detective, who specialized in rare paintings. His name was Richard Steedle, and he gave me a lift back to New York. The headlights reflected back blindingly in the fog. It was arduous driving. Steedle turned on the radio.

After the weather report, a newscaster reminded the world that 24 of our 72 hours were gone. The White House was still determined to resist any capitulation to the Haziri demands. With the antiquated 180-megabyte mag tape systems they used at SSA, I hoped they had a lot of backup already stored off-site. Every computer system should have a disaster recovery plan. I remembered my usual lecture about systems backup.

Steedle switched off the radio. "Joseph Mallord William Turner," the silver haired detective said. "Exhibited his first oil painting in 1799. He began his first impressionist style about 1830, both as to form and color. Some of his famous paintings are *Kilchurn Castle, Lock Awe, The Wreck of the Minotaur,* and *The Tenth Plague of Egypt*. Lloyd Henderson's stolen painting was called *Salvage at Sea*. Quite a provenance. Some tin magnate bought it from a French duke, then sold it to one of the big galleries. Henderson acquired it at an auction. Paid just a bit over a million for it. Worth now maybe four or five million."

"Impressionists, along with contemporary paintings, have increased twice as fast as Old Masters, according to figures by Sotheby. More than securities," I said, thinking back to a *Wall Street Journal* article I had read and my lousy university retirement plan.

"So, you know something about these paintings. Well, paintings do *not* pay dividends like the stock market. And art can be stolen a lot more easily."

"Yasuda Fire & Marine apparently charged visitors $40 a head to look at Van Gogh's *Sunflowers*, which was acquired in 1987 for $39.9 million," I replied. "The admission fees are similar to dividends."

Steedle didn't reply. He seemed to be deep in thought.

"What do you think the crooks will do with it?" I asked him.

"Oh, they may try to sell it back to Henderson through a go-between or sell it to a collector who'll stick it away in some secret hiding place and every now and then look at it and lick his chops and think he's on top of the world. His closest friends won't even know he has it. He couldn't take any chances. Or maybe they'll hide it and wait seven years for the statute of limitations to run so they can't be prosecuted. Then 'discover' it and try to collect a big reward for its return."

"I've been hearing about schemes like that," I said.

Was this like opportunity cost I thought? As I explain to my students, an opportunity cost is a benefit that is given up when one alternative is chosen over another. The foregone benefit can be either financial or non-financial. For example, a financial opportunity cost could be where a company has a vacant lot that it is leasing out as a parking lot. If the company decides to build its new office on the site, the opportunity cost would be the lost rental income from the parking lot lease.

Non-financial opportunity costs are incurred by each student that attends my evening accounting classes. In deciding to attend class after work, they have each given up something, such as eating dinner with their family, going to a movie, sleeping, going out on a date, or just having beer with their friends. For these students, the opportunity cost of attending my evening classes is whatever they gave up listening to my hopefully exciting and informative lecture. Sure, they are! The benefit foregone is a cost that usually does not appear in the financial records but is nevertheless one that is always involved in choosing between alternative uses of resources.

"Oh, they try, anyway."

"Wonder why they didn't take the whole collection?"

"That did cross my mind," he admitted. "There's one explanation. Some shady collector placed an order. He goes to a bad guy, and now he's the gloating owner of a famous Turner. The thieves took the order and took the painting this collector was wanting. Just like car stereos."

"Maybe."

"You don't buy it?"

I glanced at his profile. "No. Do you?"

"It's one explanation," he said. "Look, there's crooks who specialize in certain kinds of cars. They get an order for a model, so they go out and steal one. They bring it to their shop, and in a couple of hours the car gets chopped and re-ID'd. We just broke up an operation like that on the East Side. That doesn't mean some other gang won't set up the same thing on the West Side. If there's money in it, you'll find the crooks."

"They had to get a key," I said.

"Sure. So, they had help on the inside. One of the employees, probably. They're all being checked out. If we find one with a record, we'll watch him."

We were in Manhattan, and he offered to drop me off at my apartment. I gave him my address. We were silent until he parked in front of my building. "We'll get them," he said.

"Look, I'm going to be up for a while. You want some coffee before you go on in all this fog?"

"Hey, thanks."

Upstairs, I made some black coffee, and we sat at the kitchen table and drank it. He looked at some stuff on the walls and said I had impressive taste. I said thanks, and then I laid the story out for him. Lloyd Henderson and his daughters. The one who took off and the two who stayed.

Steedle was probably about fifty, well dressed, almost sophisticated, for a detective. "You think one of the daughters was the inside person?"

"I think so."

"Which one?"

I just shrugged and refilled our mugs.

"If one of the daughters leaves the old man and suddenly starts throwing money around we'll have her."

"There's nerve and intelligence behind this one," I said. "If one of the daughters was behind it, she isn't going to give the show away. Unless she takes a trip to South America or Europe and starts living like a queen. And then you'll have to find the painting for your proof."

Steedle made a fist, rubbed the big knuckle of his index finger on his front teeth. His brow was intense. "We still haven't found Manfred. You think he was in on the robbery? Maybe lifted the key?"

"I don't know. I think he knew it was coming."

"You haven't told me everything, have you?"

"Everything—except one thing that could get me into trouble."

He laughed. He relaxed his intent thoughts and drank some more coffee. "Why were the artists killed?"

"I think they knew what was going to happen," I said. "The robbery. The big one. I think somebody got careless and let it slip. I told you about Relgado. Sergei didn't kill the two artists. At least, I don't think he did. But he did try to scare Masters out of town—I'm fairly sure about that one."

"Wouldn't be surprised if Henderson was behind it all himself," Steedle said seriously. "He still keeps the painting, and collects four million from his insurance company," Steedle said. "Been done before."

"I thought of that one too. Henderson's got plenty of dough. But he's probably just greedy enough to try it. I don't know, maybe he's self-insured."

"Anyone else you want to rule out?" Steedle asked. I couldn't tell if he was being sarcastic or just condescending.

"Not really."

"You think Relgado led those crooks today?"

"I think they were his men."

"All we need is the proof."

"You might get it," I said. "Then again you might not. Let's hope they start fighting among themselves and blow the whole operation."

"That's a possibility," Steedle said. "But once they fall out, there's usually more shooting."

I didn't have anything to say to that one.

I took the phone off the hook after Steedle left. I didn't want to be bothered by anyone. If the Hazirians or Al-Qaeda blew up the whole world, I didn't want to hear about it. I just wanted to rent a cottage on a secluded beach for a year somewhere and do nothing but sleep on the beach at night and research during the day.

The next morning was bright and sunny. I called Tom at his apartment and asked him to pick me up. I was downstairs when he showed up in a cab. We had the driver take us to Frank Masters's place.

We went to his apartment, but he had obviously left in a hurry. Didn't even lock the door behind him.

Tom had heard about the stolen Turner. The robbery had been on the television news, even replacing news about the bomb threats. "Everything was leading up to that, huh?" he quizzed.

"I think so."

"Can you tell me why we came here?"

"To see if Masters is really gone. I guess he did disappear after all."

We left and went to the accounting office.

John Grant was waiting for me. I sat in front of his desk and listened to him and wished I had stayed home in bed.

"I have police coming out of my ears," he bellowed. "Then Henderson calls. He claims he hasn't gotten one thing out of us for his money. Look, this is a wealthy client, and we can't sell him any more accounting work if we don't come through for him on this engagement. He wants that painting back. I told him we run the best asset recovery operation in New York, and if anyone could run it down and get it back, it's us. Now look, Lenny, you'd better come up with some ideas."

I wonder what the opportunity cost of Henderson's money is to him? What would be his alternative uses for the cash he is paying Grant for this job? It isn't like he would be short on cash and must give up something else. Must be that non-financial opportunity cost. He wants to win. He wants big returns (in the form of knowledge) for his money.

"As usual we are looking for a particular needle in a bag of needles. Typical fraud engagement. Where's Henderson now?"

"In his New York office. Why?"

"Business as usual," I replied.

"What do you expect him to do, stay home and bite his nails?"

"You're right. Working keeps your mind off bad things."

"You'll come up with something, Lenny. Don't let me down."

"Right," I feigned. "And maybe pigs can fly."

Grant didn't look happy with my remark.

I went to my own office and sat down behind my desk and thought about what to do next. What moves did I have left anyway? What would a sharp forensic asset recovery investigator do?

Tom dropped in and said he'd bring up some decent coffee if I wanted it. I told him I would wait for lunch.

Two police officers arrived at the office and asked a lot of routine questions. I was courteous and told them what they needed. They finally left, but not happy though. I worked on a stale research project. The *Journal of Management Accounting Research,* an American Accounting Association academic journal, had rejected one of my research papers. I was thankful it was Spring break, and I didn't have to teach any classes for a few more days. It gave me the breather I needed to try to bring this engagement to some kind of closure. At this point I felt that my left foot did not know what my right foot was doing.

Around noon Tom and I went for lunch. Grilled steaks, baked potatoes with butter, sour cream and chives, house salads and iced tea. We sat in the back and watched a blonde toy with her food. When a man in a dark blue business suit showed up, she brightened up and became more animated.

"I wish I had a blonde like that waiting for me," Tom sighed.

"Just for lunch or for life?"

"For life," Tom said. He drank some tea. "I work crazy hours, and I don't know when I'll get a vacation."

"You're a bad prospect," I said. "Unless you get a wife who doesn't care."

"Cops' wives don't seem to mind."

"They mind, all right. The sad part is that police have a high divorce rate. Their marriages become occupational casualties."

"Didn't you ever want to get married?"

"I was married once. My wife was killed in a car accident — almost four years ago now. Drunk driver, expired license, expired registration, and no insurance. Got off almost scot-free." There goes another accounting related term, scot-free. Scot was a medieval tax. If a man managed to not have to pay it, he was scot free. Oh, the details kept in the mind of a forensic accountant.

"Sorry, I never knew that."

"Twenty percent of the drivers on the road make one payment on their insurance so they can get license plates. They never make another payment, and drive around for two years on the plates — destroying property and destroying lives. Think about all the illegals in the U.S. The motor vehicle guys just don't have enough manpower to go running around trying to get the plates back. Makes you sick."

We were walking along 42nd Street toward the office when someone walking towards us gasped and froze. She was looking beyond us. I turned and saw a car coming fast with a gun barrel sticking out of the front window. I tackled Tom, and we went down, sprawling on the sidewalk. The bullets flew over our heads. The lady who had gasped, screamed, and clutched her side. She went down. The car's tires screeched as it swerved around the next corner and raced away. Tom and I were on our feet. People had scrambled out of the way. I bent over the fallen woman. There was a lot of blood. Her face was pasty. She didn't even look 30.

Another woman ran over. "What happened?" She was middle-aged and wore an orange colored waitress uniform.

"Call an ambulance," I shouted to her.

Tom grabbed my arm. "Come on!"

We hurried away. "Could you tell who it was?" Tom asked.

"I don't know who shot at us, but it was helpful Hossein driving the car."

"Relgado's thug," Tom blistered.

"Let's get over there," I said, waving down a cab. We piled into the cab, and Tom gave the driver the address.

"You got a gun?"

"No," I said.

"Well, I have one."

The Antalya Room was closed. We stood in front of the main entrance thinking for a minute, where to go from here. "Somebody has to be inside," I said. "Cleaning or getting ready for tonight."

We found an unlocked side door. A man was behind a service bar, putting ice in a bin. He was stocky with brown hair. "Not open yet," he said.

"Is Sergei around?" I asked.

The man looked at us and decided he didn't like our looks. He put a scowl on his beefy face. "Who wants to know?"

"We do," Tom said, producing his gun. "Come on out of there," Tom ordered. "And keep your hands where I can see them."

He did as he was told, but he wasn't scared. "Hey, I just work here," he said. "You got business with Mr. Relgado, you come back later."

"Is anybody else here?" I demanded.

"No. Just me."

A car pulled up in front. There were footsteps. Somebody stuck a key in the lock.

"Get back in the kitchen," I ordered.

"Nyet," the stocky man refused.

Tom shoved him, and the man went down hitting his head on the corner of a table. We took him by the arm pits and dragged him to the back. I let him slump to the floor, then I heard their voices. Two of them. One was Hossein. "I cannot believe you missed him," Hossein kept repeating. He sounded infuriated.

"I will get him ..."

Tom and I walked out, and Hossein stiffened. He saw the gun in Tom's hand, and slowly lifted his hands. The other man was short, dark, and scrawny, and he stared sullenly at us. I extracted a pistol from each man and put them in my jacket pockets.

"Where's Relgado?" I demanded from Hossein.

"What is this, some joke?"

"Get this turkey in the back." I jerked a thumb at Hossein's partner. I took out one of the guns, a 9mm, pointed it at Hossein, as Tom marched our would-be assailant into the kitchen. I heard a crack, groan, a slumping thud, and Tom came back.

"You tried to kill us," I barked at Hossein.

"You will all die," he scoffed.

"Relgado sent you?" I said.

"What kind of game is this? You know Sergei is dead. You killed him."

I shot a quick glance at Tom and peered back at Hossein. "What?"

"You heard what I said."

"I didn't kill Relgado," I said.

Hossein was unconvinced. "American ..." he spit with contempt.

"When did Relgado get it?" Tom asked.

Hossein did some sneering, and Tom shoved the gun hard under his chin. "When?" Tom demanded like an explosive drill sergeant.

"Keep your powder dry, Tom," I said. I was the good cop.

"Last night," Hossein sputtered, "I found him at his home. Many shots in him."

"So, you put two and two together and decided I killed him," I said. "Then you and your friend came gunning for me."

"I am not afraid of you weak American," Hossein scoffed. "If you are going to shoot me, do it."

"Were you in Long Beach yesterday?"

Hossein looked at me stonily. "No."

"Where's the painting?" I insisted.

"If this guy wants to die," Tom said, "I'm about ready to help him." An empty threat, but sometimes an effective one.

"You will not kill me," Hossein sniffed.

"Just tell us where the painting is located," I said. "And nobody will hurt you."

"Sergei *had* the painting," Hossein said.

"You know what it's worth?"

"I am not a stupid American," Hossein retorted. "I look for this. I could not find it anywhere."

"Who do you think took it?" I said.

"I am not knowing this. I think *you* took it."

"I told you I didn't kill him. Was it Jeannette—the lady with the black wig?" I pressed with increasing impatience.

Tom looked at me.

"I am not knowing this," Hossein squirmed.

"Who gave the orders to steal the painting? Relgado or the woman in the black wig?"

"Both of them. They work together."

"Were you supposed to go yesterday?" I said. "Was yesterday the day for the break-in?"

"No. Something change the plan. We got orders to hit a week sooner. That was being yesterday. I ask Sergei why. He tells me shut up."

"Go, get in the men's room," I ordered.

Hossein practically fled.

"What now?" Tom said.

"Let's get out of here."

A few blocks away I called Henderson's palace on Long Island on my cell phone. I asked for Sandra and was told she wasn't there. She was probably in the city. Then I asked for Cora. She came to the phone.

"This is Lenny Cramer. I'd like to talk with you."

"Not now. My father is leaving his office early, and it's going to be bad. He's absolutely fuming over yesterday. If you want to make the trip, I can give you a few minutes. But there's nothing more I can add to what you already know."

"Uh huh. Do you know Sergei Relgado was shot last night?"

"I don't know the gentleman."

"He wasn't exactly a gentleman. I may come out there later today."

"The lady in the wig?" Tom said. "You're talking about Sandra Henderson. Where does she fit in?"

"Someday, when you come home with a good report card, I'll tell you all about it."

"Playing it close, huh? Well, I found a couple of dozen more paintings that were sold to empty storefronts. At least seven were sold to the same three or four addresses. Is Sandra the inside lady?"

"Figured it out, huh?" We started walking.

"One day Sandra stumbles over the key to the room where the paintings are kept. She lifts the key, then borrows Paul Manfred's gun. Has a copy made and gives the copy to her buddy Relgado. Sandra was behind it all along. Did she knock off Relgado too?" Tom reasoned.

"We know some of it," I said. "Not all of it."

"Go ahead and keep me in the dark. See if I care."

"The bad guys are falling out. I wonder who is going to end up with the jackpot?" I said.

We took a cab to Marilyn's place in SoHo and found that Marilyn and Myra were both there. Myra greeted me warmly, and Tom gazed with mock appreciation. I took Myra aside, and Tom began talking with Marilyn.

"Who do you think has the Turner painting?" I asked Myra.

Myra made her eyes round. "I don't know."

"I'm going to Long Beach," I said. "Why don't we all go together?"

Myra frowned. "You know I can't go there."

"I don't think your father will make a scene when he hears what I have to say," I pronounced confidently. "There's been a lot of upheaval. His pride and joy are gone. He may never see it again. Come on, Myra, this may be a chance ... if nothing else you can do a little gloating."

Marilyn was annoyed. "That's horrible."

"Yes," Tom said, as he came out from the hallway. "That's a horrible thing to say." He patted Marilyn on the back of the shoulder. He was paying her quite a bit of attention.

Was it May yet? I didn't think it was. Couldn't be. Spring break wasn't over yet. One day just seemed to blur into another. I figured it was the last day of April or the first day of May. What did it matter? There was a time during my Ph.D. program when I really wasn't sure which year it was. I was sure the Haziris knew which year it was. And it was day eight out of ten.

"We're going to Long Beach." I was adamant. "Now come on. Let's go."

Downstairs, we waited for a cab.

The second taxi to drive down the street looked empty, and we stopped it. Everyone piled in. I told the driver where we wanted to go. He balked. In fact, he was just heading back to his dispatcher. I stuffed a 20-dollar bill in his hand. "That's on top of whatever the meter says." He conceded, and we headed for Long Beach.

When we arrived, Lloyd Henderson was upstairs in his sitting room and wasn't likely to come down till dinner time. So, Cora told me. She looked coldly at Myra and Marilyn.

"It's old home week," I told Cora. "I insisted they come along. I hate traveling alone."

Cora looked at me like I was an insect. "What are you meddling with now, Dr. Cramer?"

"I just wanted to see the family all together," I said. The others weren't paying attention to us. Sandra had entered the room. Eyes made of dry ice. Silent. I took Sandra's arm, and we strolled through the formal garden by the side of the house. "Who's got the painting, Sandra?"

"How should I know, Dr. Cramer," she said, venomously amused, haughty.

"Sergei Relgado had it last. Somebody killed him for it. Who could get close to him without him getting suspicious? Some woman in a black wig?"

"Those are your questions, Dr. Cramer, so why don't *you* answer them?"

"It was more than just stealing a painting, wasn't it," I said. We stopped walking, and we stood face to face, under a maple tree, and behind her was a row of spring plants. "You and your sisters hate your father. You wanted out of here, so you hatched a perfect plan, didn't you. Why not strike at the source of your pain, and destroy what he treasured most? The Turner painting. You had it all planned out perfectly, even to the day. But I put a crimp in your plans. I found out what the target was. It was the Turner, and you couldn't wait the extra week. You moved the day I discovered what the real painting was. And the only person who knew that was Myra."

"And Myra informed us, so we went ahead with the plan the very same day," Sandra cooed, with haughty superiority. "You have it all figured out, don't you? How clever. I won't add or subtract a thing Lenny. It's your story. Now all you have to do is prove it."

The bitterness seethed like a scorpion's poison. Cold, calculating, and bent on vindictiveness. The sins of the father? "There's three murders, Sandra. Somebody must pay."

"Sometimes you ring up the cash register and it says, 'No Sale.'"

Her smug arrogance gave me a sick feeling in the pit of my stomach. "Where's Paul Manfred?"

"Paul who?" she feigned.

"Your game is over, Sandra."

"Is it? We'll see." She leaned toward me. "You will stay for dinner, won't you? You and your charming friend? I'll arrange it with father."

"He's liable to throw you out."

Sandra patted my cheek. "How can that bother me if I have $4 million in my hands? Or will have? Isn't that what you think?"

We went back to the porch, and Tom took me inside the house. "I've got a gun in my pocket, wrapped up in a handkerchief. Spotted it at Marilyn's while you were busy talking. But what if it's not the gun that killed Sergei? Marilyn will know I took it. You'll have to do some explaining."

"Don't worry about it."

Lloyd Henderson declined to come down for dinner, so one of the staff took him a tray. Before we left I went up to his sitting room. It was an enormous room, and he looked lost in it. He scowled at me. "Why did you bring Myra here? You know she's not welcome in my house. And I can barely tolerate that Marilyn."

"I thought you had a soft spot for Marilyn?" I stood by the side of his posh, leather recliner. His eyes were sunken, but alive and animated. He was a tough old bird.

"Just a spark," he murmured. "Just a small spark." He twisted his head and looked up at me. "What about my painting?"

"Sergei Relgado had it last. He's dead, and someone else has it now. One double-cross after another."

"You will get it back for me. Won't you?"

Somehow, I almost felt sorry for him. Then again, I wasn't his kid. I told him I was a forensic accountant. He hired me to investigate Marilyn's alleged financial chicanery at her mother's art gallery. I told him how fake paintings were being sold to non-existent customers. About my suspicions of drug money being transferred to Relgado in the form of fictitious loan repayments. He shook his head angrily and muttered something that sounded like a combination of contempt and abject frustration. I left him to his misery.

Sandra drove Marilyn, Myra, Tom, and me to the station, and didn't wait for the train to arrive. She waved her hand, and drove back to the house, back to her father.

When we got to Grand Central, I hailed another cab for the mother and daughter, told Myra I might call her later, and then Tom and I went back to the office. Only the night man was there, reading a magazine, *New Accountant*, with a picture of a forensic accountant on the front cover. But not me. Said his daughter was studying accounting at NYU. A good profession. I agreed.

We went into my office.

Tom unwrapped the gun on my desk. It was a .38 caliber Smith & Wesson revolver. He put a pencil through the barrel and lifted the gun. Several bullets were missing. Looked at the spent powder on the edge of the chamber and sniffed it. "Yep," he said. Which meant it'd been recently fired.

I wrapped the gun up and locked it in a drawer of my desk. "You owe me a handkerchief," Tom said.

"Where'd you find it?"

"In a linen drawer under some towels in the bathroom," Tom said matter-of-factly.

"Let's talk."

"Sure." Tom settled in the client's chair in front of my desk.

"You found the gun in Marilyn's apartment, so Marilyn gets the prize … unless her mother planted the gun there. But I doubt it. Daughters will throw their own mothers to the wolves, but mothers are a certain breed. It's not likely a mother would sell her own daughter down the river."

"Where does that put Sandra? Or Jeannette?"

"Sandra is right there, up to her claws in murder and grand larceny. I don't know if she actually pulled the trigger, but she was behind it, all right."

"And what about Cora?"

"She's in on it too."

Tom shook his head. "You're guessing."

"If the gun you found today is the murder weapon, the one that killed Relgado, then Marilyn will talk. Even part of a print should do the trick."

"Who killed Noren and Walker?"

"I think it was Marilyn."

"Killed her own lover?" Tom was skeptical.

"There were millions involved," I told Tom. "Marilyn's share would come to at least a million or more. When people are into drugs, they become irrational, and desperate." I rubbed the back of my aching neck.

"The artists knew what they were doing with the fake paintings, and I think they knew about the sisters' plan," I said. "Either Marilyn slipped and told them about the theft, or maybe she was trying to maneuver them to be the fall guys for the theft. On the other hand, maybe they were all abusing the men in their lives, just as their father used and abused them over the years."

"You're still guessing."

"It fits. You checked it out. You told me there was no stealing from the gallery, only signs of using it to launder the drug money."

Tom grimaced. "Some Columbo—trench coat and all. It fits nicely, so it must be true."

"You go and talk to Shirley. I want to talk to Myra, without Marilyn around."

After Tom left I dialed Myra's number. She answered on the fourth ring. "You're alone?"

"Yes. Marilyn went home an hour ago."

"What's with Marilyn?"

"She—uh—doesn't feel well."

"Something she ate ... or drank?"

"Your friend, Tom—did he search through Marilyn's apartment?" she asked.

"A little."

"I see." There was a tense pause. "What are you going to do?"

"I thought I'd come over and talk to you."

"All right, Lenny."

I slowly hung up the receiver, thought for a moment, switched off the light, and left my office.

# Fifteen

*Performance standards are essential to a management principle known as* management by exception, *which states that management should devote its scarce time only to operations in which results depart significantly from the performance standards.*

—Gordon Shillinglaw

Myra tried to look calm, but her hands were trembling. She poured coffee into mugs from a ceramic pot. We sat in the living room, and her eyes studied me. "Marilyn didn't kill Sergei or anyone," she said. "I did it. I did it myself."

"Sure."

"I was with you when you found out that the Joseph Turner painting was what we were after. I warned Sandra and Cora, and so they had the robbery done that same day."

"But you were the one who *told* me about the Turner," I reminded her. "You didn't really want the robbery to take place, did you. You thought if the others knew I'd found out, they'd call it off. But they didn't."

I sipped some coffee which tasted good. "How could they? They were in too deep already, with two murders on their hands. And it wasn't greed that was driving them. It was hate. Hate and 30 years of pent up resentment against a father that treated all of you with disrespect, like trash under his feet. A father that gave the love and acceptance you needed to corroding relics and to his own idols. I thought you were in it too, Myra. But no. Your father gave you a raw deal, but you didn't hate him. Despite how much he rejected you, he was still your father. The others though—Cora and Sandra. They were going to make him pay. And they had a willing ally in Marilyn."

"You don't know what you're saying," she protested.

"I'm sorry, Myra. I'm no shrink. I'm just calling it like I see it. You didn't want Marilyn to get involved with it. You asked your father for help, hoping some private eye or lawyer would be able to stop them. Instead he called me. I'm sorry I didn't get to the real issues sooner. I was thrown off by the ruse about Marilyn stealing assets from your art gallery. It's not easy to fight family hatred and greed. Cora and Sandra wanted revenge. They were sick of looking after your father—giving, giving, giving, and being stepped on like insignificant fools in return—day in and day out, year in and year out, for over 30 years. You were stronger though. You left before it got the better of you. They didn't. They must hate him beyond what you and I can possibly imagine."

"Not a good enough motive," Myra said.

"A good analogy is the make-or-buy decision in cost accounting. The relevant cost information for making a product consists of the short-term costs to produce it, generally the variable manufacturing costs, which would be saved if the product is purchased. These costs are compared to the purchase prices of the needed product to determine the appropriate decision."

"What?" Myra looked confused.

"Look, they could sit around for years waiting for Dad to die. Actually, it's a make, lease, or buy decision. They could buy the painting today by stealing it. Or they could lease living in the house until Henderson dies. But suppose he decided to donate much of his wealth to Columbia University? They were not willing to take that chance."

She lifted the mug of coffee and then set it down. Her eyes were wet. "I can't believe it all got so out of hand." She was trying to hold back from weeping. Teddy and Bram were never even part of it, and now they're dead. She gulped. Tried to hold staccato breaths. "I'm not going to worry about that Sergei Relgado. He got my daughter into this drug business. Marilyn got in with the wrong crowd, and it's all my fault, Lenny." She couldn't hold back any longer and was convulsing with tears.

"You think it's that simple? Come on, Myra. Your sisters and your daughter made their own choices. Make, lease, or buy. They took their chances, and they lost. Where's the painting now?"

"I don't know," she said in a resigned whisper.

"It's got to be hidden somewhere."

"You want to search my apartment, Lenny? Go ahead," she said with all the injured pride she could muster.

"It wouldn't be here," I said. "They don't trust you anymore, do they?"

"They knew how I felt. But what was I supposed to do?" Her face was distraught, strain around her eyes. "Report my sisters and my own daughter to the police?" She retorted. She was starting to lose it. "There was nothing I could do."

I didn't argue with her. Three murders. Up to their eye balls in crime. And there was nothing she could do. I drank some coffee, but it now tasted bitter. I put the mug down. "Do you think they'll brazen it out?"

"I don't know," she shook her head, looking down. Her whole body was shaking.

Her eyes glistened with tears. Her mascara was black streaks running down her cheeks.

"It was Cora and Sandra. They talked Marilyn into going along."

"Did Marilyn let it slip to the artists," I said. "Is that what happened? Or did she hate Teddy as well—was he abusing her—or was she abusing *him*? I don't imagine he was a strong personality."

"One night after a wild party Marilyn was high—almost out of her mind. Bram was there. She told the story to Teddy in front of him. The next day she knew she'd made a mistake and went to Sandra. It was Sandra who decided Teddy and Bram had to be silenced."

"And Marilyn obliged," I finished sarcastically. "Easy enough for her to kill her love-hate, crack-head boyfriend. And then Bram Walker had to go. Why did she stop there? Why didn't she kill Masters too?" Myra was sobbing heavily, unable to talk. I put my arm around her. Held her for a few seconds.

"Frank wasn't there the night Marilyn told about the robbery. But Teddy or Bram might have told him, so Sandra had Sergei try to scare Frank out of the country." She dropped her face into her graceful, sweating hands.

"Then Marilyn killed Sergei," I pressed on. "She took the painting. What did she do with it?"

"I don't know. I don't know," she insisted, crying now without control. "I asked her. She wouldn't tell me. She probably gave it to Sandra or Cora."

"They wouldn't keep it in the house on Long Beach. They're not that stupid."

"I don't know where it is Lenny. Honestly, I don't." She struggled to regain some composure.

"All right, Myra." I put my arm firmly around her. "Marilyn's a big girl." I took her by the shoulders and looked directly into her face. "She went into this scheme with her eyes open. Time value of money. A dollar today is worth much more than a dollar ten year from now. She was looking for the big bucks today and thought she could trash anyone that stood in her way. But it didn't work." I stood up slowly. "There are no winners in this game, Myra. Only losers."

She didn't see me to the door.

The next morning, in my apartment I started on the phone. I finally located Detective Richard Steedle. I asked him to meet me in my office in an hour. He agreed. There was something about him I respected a lot. He was a straight shooter, and he understood the issues.

I shaved and showered and was in my office in 40 minutes. When he arrived, I gave him the gun. "I think it was used to kill Sergei Relgado. That'll be up to your folks in ballistics. There may be prints on it. Marilyn Riley is the one you'll want. She also killed the two artists."

"You'd better give it to me straight, Cramer," he said.

And I did. I laid out the whole sordid mess to him. It had finally come to a head. And everything was pouring out in torrents. Cora, Sandra, and Marilyn—I talked about the hate, the greed, and the murders. Steedle took the gun away, after talking about concrete evidence. It was now up to ballistics and the fingerprint experts.

I sank into a slow depression. Reminded me of a bumper sticker I saw on a car yesterday: "Gravity Gets Me Down." It scared me to think I'd started getting sucked into the whole web of lies and manipulation myself. Tom was right—I was being played like a violin, suckered into withholding evidence, misleading everyone, including myself, thinking I was helping my client. The velvet claws are subtle, and I realized I was no more immune than the next well-meaning sap.

Hildy dropped a fax on my desk but stayed away. She saw my mood.

Tom came in later and talked about Shirley. He'd talked with her late last night.

"The poor kid's out of a job now," he informed me sympathetically. "The Antalya's closed down. I told her she'd make a great administrative secretary."

"That would be an experience, wouldn't it?" I said flatly.

"What are you moping around for?"

I told him that I'd dumped the whole thing on Richard Steedle.

"And you're convinced Myra wasn't part of the whole scheme?" He sounded skeptical.

"Yeah. I really don't think so."

"You sure you're not just swayed by your feelings for her? You'd feel like a real sucker if you find out she was just trying to save her own hide, playing you for a fool."

I said nothing.

Tom sat down and stretched out his long legs. "You're a smart accountant, Lenny. Real smart. Even for a Ph.D. But you have a sentimental streak that'll get you into trouble every time in this profession."

I looked up at the corner of the ceiling. I saw that the spider's web was gone. Someone must have noticed it and used a broom.

I wondered if the spider was dead. If it was the stubborn kind, and might still be alive and kicking, it would build another web again—somewhere.

Could Lloyd Henderson rebuild his web without his daughters? He was no dummy. He knew they hated him. Did he even suspect they were behind the theft of his painting?

* * *

There was a memo from Hildy on my desk after Tom and I came back from lunch the next day. I returned the call and found myself talking to Richard Steedle.

"The homicide boys called me. They can work fast when they feel like it. Ballistics checked out the gun. You can pick one up on the street for fifty dollars. The bullet that killed Sergei came from that gun, and the prints on it belong to Marilyn Riley. An assistant D.A. is getting a warrant. Can't do anything about Cora and Sandra Henderson unless Marilyn sings. Are you sure Myra Riley is out of the picture?"

"I'm sure."

"And the painting?"

"Maybe Marilyn will confess. I don't know. Can't even guess. We got a fax from Sotheby's—confirms one of the paintings sold through Myra's gallery couldn't possibly have been real. Different owners, different buyers, and different prices. All within the time Sotheby's had possession of the original."

"Well, my crew gave Relgado's place—the Antalya Room—a complete shake down. From top to bottom. No paintings. No forgeries. But some other interesting stuff. Five hundred kilos of crack, some cases of wax, and expensive laboratory scales. Oh, and a small arsenal of automatic weapons, and what looks like high tech electronic gizmos. All of it was in the basement. And something else. Maybe you can help us on this one. We found boxes full of Relgado's financial records. I'd appreciate it if you'd look them over and let us know if you find anything that might help. Relgado's murder has nothing to do with me. I'm only assigned to recover that painting. I have two or three good informants on the street. So far, nothing. That Turner painting is being kept out of sight."

"Sure, be glad to help with the records. That painting will show up."

"They don't always show up," Steedle said. "There are millionaire collectors in Europe and South America. They thrive on owning rare art—something no one else can have."

"Let me know if Marilyn gives a full confession, will you?"

"As soon as I get the word, I'll call you."

"If I'm not here, I'll be at home." I hung up and sat down. It wasn't long before one of Steedle's junior officers delivered a hand truck load of cardboard boxes into my office. He got my signature and left. They were dusty. Most police departments don't have forensic auditors or the budget money to hire forensic auditors. I filled out a standard engagement letter and faxed it to Steedle

I sighed, and started to pull the file folders out, to begin organizing what I had. Bank statements ... cash register receipts ... purchase invoices ... utility bills. I picked up a folder and noticed what looked like a stack of letters to some federal agency in it.

I thumbed through the letters. They all looked the same, just different names. I picked one up and read it. I quickly fanned through the stack—there must have been a hundred of them. I picked up one of the bank statements and calculated a couple of quick ratios. Then I dug frantically through the box until I found a payroll register. Names, names.... Darn! There was no time to match them all, but one thing was sure, there wasn't a fraction of them on the Antalya's payroll. As I raced out the door I yelled to Hildy, "Call Steedle *now*! Tell him I'll be at the Antalya in twenty minutes! *Urgent!*"

I nearly got killed running in front of a cab to get it to stop. I barked out the address as I got in and slammed the door. We raced to the Antalya Room. I shoved a twenty-dollar bill in the driver's hand and dashed to the Antalya's front door. I barged my way in and found Steedle. "Look, we have to move fast, the 72 hours is almost up!" I shouted.

"What are you talking about?" Steedle thought I was nuts.

The payroll ... look there's no time. Where are those gizmos? I was almost frantic.

Steedle and I ran down the dirty wood stairs to the basement, and he showed me the devices he had mentioned. A *box* of them. They almost looked like telephone pagers. "Find a screwdriver!" I shouted.

One of the officers picked one up off a utility shelf near the furnace and handed it to me. "No! No! Phillips! Phillips! It's the wrong kind!" I ran over to the shelf and rummaged like a lunatic throwing electrical fixtures and small tools out of my way.

"Got it!" I ran back and grabbed one of the gizmos. I carefully unscrewed the back-cover plate. "Look at this!" I said to Steedle.

He peered inside. "Is that what I think it is?" he asked, eyebrows arched high.

"You bet! Look, get on your radio. Tell them to let the demolition guys down in Baltimore know what we've got here," I almost ordered him. I looked at the circuit board inside it again. Some of the memory chips were lithographed with a white LHE logo. LHE ... Lloyd Henderson Enterprises ...

Steedle went out to his car carrying the open gizmo. I followed him out and went around the back of the Antalya to snoop around some more. Behind the kitchen entrance was a wooden fence that wrapped around a smelly garbage dumpster. I walked behind it into the alleyway and saw some battered old garbage cans leaning next to a rusty bulkhead. It was attached to the foundation of the building.

Odd? I mused. Tire tracks backed up to the bulkhead. I hadn't remembered seeing a bulkhead entrance when I was in the basement. It had a padlock on the handle. I went back to Steedle's car and asked him to let me take the tire iron out of his trunk. I went back to the bulkhead.

After a few minutes of twisting and wrestling with the lock, I managed to skin my knuckles twice, and whacked my arm with the tire iron when it slipped. I was getting angry now. I wedged the tire iron under the hasp and kicked it with all my weight. The hasp let go, and I opened the bulkhead.

Concrete stairs led down half a flight to a small, musty room. It was cool. In the dusky shadows I could make out some wooden boxes of lettuce stacked against one wall. There were boxes of empty liquor bottles stacked against another. Humph. They're supposed to smash those, so the bottles don't get reused, I muttered to myself. Don't imagine they cared much about compliance with laws and regulations. The floor was filthy. Strewn with decaying lettuce leaves, and who knows what other garbage. Wouldn't be surprised if there were rats down here. At the back of the room was the door to a walk-in refrigerator.

I found the light switch to the walk-in and turned it on. Then I opened the door and went inside. It was *cold*. As I started ripping open cardboard case boxes to see what I could find, I thought I heard rats scurrying. Just then I spotted the corner of.... Slam! The walk-in door shut behind me, and the lights went out. I heard footsteps running up the stairs and the steel bulkhead door crashed shut.

"Hey!" I shouted. I jerked the inside door handle up and down frantically and kept on shouting. No use. Something was jamming it. It was pitch black inside. Ohhhh ... shoot. I thought. This place is going to get cold real fast. I sure hope Steedle finds me back here before I'm frozen solid, like one of those stiffs on the gurney's I inventoried back in the hospital morgue as a junior accountant. I was terrified.

* * *

Richard Steedle's police radio was connected through to the FBI demolition team in Baltimore. As they asked questions, Steedle gave them a detailed description of the electronic gizmo. It was a state-of-the-art remote detonator. Programmable to almost any command specification.

"Unbelievable," the team leader crackled back on the radio. "How in the world did they get their hands on a box of those? They can probably set those things off from anywhere in a fifty-mile radius, based on any condition code."

Steedle read off the serial numbers that were on the chips inside the detonator. The FBI would trace their production source and widen their surveillance net around the Social Security Administration buildings.

As he finished his call, a taxi pulled up and Tom Reardon climbed out.

"Where's Lenny?" he asked.

Steedle grunted. "Try the basement." He motioned his finger toward the front door of the Antalya.

Tom looked around the main dining room, reminiscing about his visit the night Sandra-Jeannette made her debut ... and he'd met Shirley. Went downstairs. Tom asked someone, "Anyone know why Lenny was in such a hurry?" he asked. The officer who found Lenny the wrong kind of screwdriver showed him the box of remote detonators and explained our discovery. "Wheeeet, wheeeeew ..." he whistled. "Relgado was better connected than I thought."

Tom went back upstairs, and out front to Steedle. "Listen, if we can run down the plate numbers for Relgado's vehicles, maybe we can pick them up somewhere between here and Baltimore," Tom said.

Steedle called in the request to the Motor Vehicle Bureau, and he told them it was urgent. "Could be hours before we get anything," he resigned.

"I'm going to look around some more," Tom said. His cell phone chirped. It was Hildy.

"Did you catch up with Lenny?" she asked anxiously.

"He's supposed to be around here somewhere," Tom replied. "Haven't seen him yet."

"I took a look at the files he was going through before he ran out of here. He had the payroll ledger for the Antalya Room on his desk. And a file filled with employment letters. Looks like he was figuring something on one of the bank statements too."

"Employment letters?"

"Yes, must be a hundred of them," she said matter-of-factly.

"What for?" Tom asked.

"It looks like they're all addressed to the Department of Immigration and Naturalization. Let me see … blah, blah, blah … hmmmp!"

"What do they say?" Tom was getting impatient.

"They just say, 'this is to confirm that so-and-so has a firm offer of full-time employment with the Antalya Room Restaurant Corporation, blah, blah, blah.'" She read. There's a pile of them. They're all the same. All the names look Middle Eastern to me.

"Why would Lenny get so excited over that information?" Tom asked. "I thought the company was clean as a whistle."

"Beats me," Hildy replied. "Maybe something to do with illegal aliens showing employment in the U.S. so they can get visas."

"All Middle Eastern names?" Tom wondered.

"That's what they look like to me."

"Are they all on the payroll?" Tom asked.

"Hang on. This may take a few minutes." Hildy began matching the employment letters with the payroll ledger. There actually weren't more than a couple of dozen employees—a manager, an assistant manager, a bookkeeper, two chefs, four dish washers, a couple of kitchen boys, two head waiters, waiters and waitresses, bouncers, door men, bus boys…. "Ah, guess what,"

Hildy said. "I've got a way to go yet, but so far not one name matches up. It looks like none of them are really on the payroll."

"Waaaaait a minute." Tom's gears were turning. It was as if an alarm clock had gone off. "What was on the news—about those Haziri terrorists getting into the States through Canada? Wow! Double wow! Try this one on. They make it to Canada. Then Relgado gives them invitations and job letters so they can come into the States. They work out of his basement here at the Antalya Room. Look, go to the OFAC Internet site. Office of Foreign Asset Control. See if the company is on the bad company list. It is the so-called Clinton's list of bad companies. Many, many companies. Oh, by the way, guess what they found here."

"What?"

"High-tech detonators. A whole box of them. Just like the ones the Haziris probably used when they blew up that subway tunnel," Tom concluded.

"And today is the last day of their countdown!" Hildy realized. "It was all over the news last night. Our 72 hours is up. They're going to blow up the Social Security buildings, *today*."

"I'd better look around a little more for Lenny," Tom said. He hung up and put the cell phone in his pocket. He asked Steedle if Lenny might have mentioned going anywhere else.

"No. But he better bring back my tire iron," Steedle huffed.

"Tire iron?"

"Yeah. Said he needed it to break a lock open. Some basement door," Steedle added.

Tom went back down into the basement. No doors. In or out. Just the stairs. He went back up to the dining room. Then wandered into the kitchen. No Lenny Cramer, anywhere to be found.

The kitchen smelled like rancid grease or was that burned shish kabob. Tom opened the bread warmer and picked out a dinner roll. "Hard as a rock," he said to himself, and tossed it back. He walked to the back door and opened it for some fresh air. Leaned against the door frame, wondering.

The kitchen door opened out into an alley. There was a low wooden deck area outside the door, with a dilapidated fence next to it. Tom wandered out to look at what was on the other side of the fence. Garbage dumpster. Nothing in the alley. As he turned to head back into the kitchen, something caught his eye next to some old garbage cans, lying on the ground. He walked toward the garbage cans and picked it up. A tire iron. Humph. Maybe it's Steedle's.

Lenny must've dropped it. Tom thought. He walked back to the front of the building. "This yours?" he asked Steedle.

"Looks like it. Except it was not so scratched up like that." He seemed only slightly annoyed.

"Found it in the back alley," Tom reported.

"I hate when people borrow my tools and don't return them."

"Yeah, I know what you mean," Tom said. "It drives me crazy when Lenny borrows my notebook computer and keeps it for three weeks until I bug him enough to get it back."

"Did you find him?" Steedle asked.

"No. Any idea where he might be?"

"He just said something about opening a basement door," Steedle remembered.

"I looked. There's no doors in the basement."

"Oh well. Look, I have to get back to the station."

Tom headed inside the Antalya.

"Hey, maybe try out back. I think he was out there a while ago," Steedle offered as he got into his car to leave.

Tom went back to the alleyway where he'd found Steedle's tire iron. He walked past the old garbage cans. A glint of something shiny reflected from near the wall. He walked closer. Some scraped and twisted metal, on a rusty old bulkhead door. Someone had recently pried the lock off. Tom opened the door and went cautiously down the steps. "Lenny?" he called. No answer. Tom shuffled slowly as his eyes adjusted to the dark. He felt cardboard boxes. Felt things squish and crunch under his feet as he stepped. "Lenny?" he called more softly this time.

As his eyes widened, Tom could barely make out the door to a walk-in refrigerator. He felt around for a handle. There was a piece of a wooden crate stuck under the handle. Tom wiggled the stick out and opened the walk-in door. It was dark inside. He jumped back startled, as something heavy fell on his feet. "Lenny!" He gasped.

It was me all right, I just didn't know it then. Tom dragged my half-frozen body up the stairs. I was unconscious. I had no idea for how long. He hit his cell phone and called an ambulance.

A few hours later I awoke at Sinai hospital. Man, I hate the cold. I could live on the equator and still be cold. I still remember my wonderful vacation on the Galapagos Islands off the coast of Ecuador. I just baked in the sunshine.

"I thought we lost you," Tom said, standing next to me.

Hildy was there too. "What'd you think you were, Batman chasing Mr. Freeze?"

"Somebody locked me in. What time is it?" I wheezed, trying to sit up. I was perplexed.

"You're not going anywhere," Hildy said with a determined grin.

"In the walk-in. I, I—" My head reeled, and I had to lie back again.

"I heard from Steedle. You really saved the day, Lenny. The FBI got a report in on a black van with New York plates headed up the Baltimore beltway, near Security Boulevard. It looked like its springs were badly overloaded. We had the police run a check on all Relgado's plate numbers. The van checked out. It was one of his. When they pulled 'em over, there was a small fight. Your friend Hossein and two other Hazirian Liberation Army would-be bombers are now history. Was a miracle they didn't blow the whole van. It was packed from top to bottom with fifty-five-gallon drums filled with chemical explosives. You were right about the detonators. And by the way, guess where they came from."

"Where?" I mustered a sound.

"A not-to-be-named maximum-security defense contractor plant right here on Long Island."

"Not Fort Worth?" I asked, thinking of the Rick Mannino's thermos filcher.

"Nope. One of the Haziris received a clearance as a maintenance worker and wheedled his way into a secure area."

"How did they find that out? I asked.

"That stack of employment letters you spotted," Tom said proudly. "It led to the name of every single Hazirian operative Relgado has brought into the country. They were all on his payroll."

"But they *weren't* on the payroll," Hildy insisted. "I checked."

"Not the Antalya payroll," I wheezed. "The drug payroll. Sergei was using the drug operation to finance the terrorist activities *inside* the U.S. That's why all the cash never showed up on any currency reporting forms or electronic funds transfer monitors. It never left the country." I was feeling a little less frozen. "And the chips. All Lloyd Henderson Enterprises?" I asked.

"Yep again. Best chips on the market," Tom crowed.

* * *

The house physician at Sinai discharged me several hours later, with strict instructions on how to treat post hypothermia. Must keep that patient length of stay short or no reimbursement.

Tom and Hildy went back to my place with me.

It was so neatly tied up. All I had to do was pick up my icicles and go home. Some forensic cost accounting case. That is, *if* Marilyn talked.

And if she did talk, then what? Cora and Sandra would be rounded up. Then a trial by jury. No guarantee they would even be convicted. Sharp lawyers can sway juries.

My part was over.

Or was it?

The painting. The Turner. Recovering missing assets. That is part of what we do.

"Wait," I remembered. "The walk-in. I have to go back."

"Are you nuts!" Hildy exclaimed. "You must have icicles on the brain."

"I thought I saw it."

"Saw what?" Tom and Hildy both chimed in together.

"The Turner!"

We went back out and took a cab to the Antalya. Straight back to the bulkhead. This time Tom went in first. Hildy and I followed. I really didn't want to go inside the walk-in, so I guarded the door, while Tom rummaged through every square inch of the refrigerator.

"Not a sign of it. It is not here."

"It has got to be here," I insisted. "I saw something behind that stack of boxes full of green peppers. Over there." I pointed to the back corner. "Behind the shelf. It looked like a rolled up, something, wrapped in brown paper."

Tom looked again, but there was no trace of anything rolled up. Brown paper or no brown paper. And nothing behind the shelf.

"Maybe whoever locked you in came back and took it," Hildy said.

"Or maybe you were just delirious," Tom concluded. "You were in there a long time."

"Well, maybe. But I could swear I saw something just before the door slammed."

"Well, let's get out of here before the door slams again. I'm freezing in here," Tom shivered.

We went back to the office, empty handed.

I picked up the phone and called Myra. "You'd better go over to Marilyn's. She's going to need you for moral support."

"I'll always hate you for this, Lenny Cramer."

She said it in a steady voice. No hysterics. She meant it. Why?

"Talk to her, Myra. Find out what she did with that painting."

"That's all you care about," she snapped, sounding hurt.

I didn't need this. "It could help her with the judge." Who was I kidding? Three cold-blooded murders. Like I had any sway, anyhow.

"You're just looking out for your client," she reasoned, sounding betrayed. "You don't care about Marilyn ... you don't even care about me."

"Okay. Look, I've been half frozen to death. Just stay away from her then."

She slammed the phone down.

I was feeling some of her pain, on top of my own. It stung, and I felt alone in that office, with not even the spider for company any more. An hour later I said good-bye to Hildy and Tom and went home.

I took my cell phone into the bathroom and got into my Jacuzzi. Hot water jets cascaded the top of my head, the back of my neck in the tub, and I tried to just put it all out of my wearied mind. When the phone rang it was Myra, not Steedle.

"I just saw Marilyn." Her breathing was heavy. "There was no painting in Sergei's apartment. They'd had a fight, a shouting match—that's when she took the gun out and shot him. She told me."

"Did the police get there yet?"

"I—I don't know. Marilyn just ran out and took off. I went after her, but I couldn't catch her."

"Where are you now?"

"In a booth on the street. Uh, ... Prince Street."

"You'd better get home. If the police talk to you, please don't mention that we talked."

"Why should I do you any favors?"

I could lose my tenured job at the university. "You can't hate me that much Myra. You did go to see Marilyn like I asked you."

"Yes. I—I don't know what to do."

It sounded like she really didn't know what to do. "Go home Myra. Stay out of it as much as you possibly can at this point. You can't help Marilyn now."

She hung up, and I got out of the tub. Dried off, put on my blue sweat suit, and gave up any idea of eating dinner. I was hungry, but I didn't want to eat anything. I sat in front of the TV set. I didn't turn it on. I just sat there and stared at it.

I shouldn't have called Myra. If she talked, the police might think I had used her to warn Marilyn. I was in trouble if they thought that. Stupid mistakes. The road to hell is paved with good intentions. The better idea is not to make the mistakes in the first place. That's not always easy.

It was late when someone rang my door bell. I got up and opened the door. Richard Steedle walked into my foyer. We sat down, and he didn't look so friendly.

"Two detectives went to get Marilyn Riley," he told me laconically. "Guess what? She'd flown the coop. One overnight bag gone. They caught up with her at the Port Authority. Hauled her over to the D.A.'s office. In half an hour she told them everything. Almost like she thought it was all a big joke. Like she thought she could get off with impunity. Her aunts are being picked up right now. They chased down some judge to issue the warrants."

"All's well that ends well," I said with a feeble grin, feeling like my face was made of scrambled eggs.

"I'd like to know how she knew we were coming to arrest her?" he said looking right at me.

"That's easy," I said. "She knew Tom found her gun, and she knew we would turn it into the police. So, she took off. What else would she do?"

Steedle seemed to relax after that. But you can't be sure with the police. They're trained in interview techniques, especially one as sharp as Steedle. He went on, "I talked to her myself about the Turner painting. She said it wasn't in Relgado's apartment. Maybe. My detectives went all over it, up and down. No painting. Could be she got the painting and stashed it with someone else."

"Know what I think?"

"What?"

"I think Relgado was double-crossing the sisters and their niece. Why should he do the dirty work, then split three or four million bucks with them?"

Steedle shook his head. "What have we here? Three dead men and a missing painting. Plus, the three Hazirians," he added. "Thanks for the tip, by the way.

That was a darn good piece of work. I'd have never figured out how to read those ledgers in time. And if it wasn't for you, we might not have connected those detonator gizmos to the Hazirians for days, maybe weeks. So, when are you going to spill everything else?" he said.

"Thanks. It just didn't take that many employees to meet the service volume for the Antalya Room. Even a quick check of the cash deposits for a month, divided by an estimated average tab for a table, showed a turnover rate nowhere near what you'd get from 100 employees. He just didn't have that many tables in the place. Basic labor budgeting," I explained. "You ought to take my course in cost accounting sometime. And look, I'm not holding out on you. Why should I?"

"I won't push it—for now." We walked to the door and shook hands, and he went away. I finished a flat can of Coke and went to bed. My head felt like I'd crashed into a brick wall.

* * *

"The last roundup," Hildy said when I walked in the next morning. "It was all over the cable news and on the front page of the papers. Hazirian Liberation Army is kaput. Cora and Sandra Henderson and Marilyn Riley—the police have them all locked up. But wait, there's more. Lloyd Henderson called early this morning to talk to Johnny. Our firm has been fired. We got the pink slip."

"I hope Grant is not too broken hearted over it," I said, and went into my office.

"There's a memo on your desk," she called after me. "Phone message."

I picked up the slip of paper. All it said was Washington Square Park—12:00.

I sat down, leaned back, and rubbed my eyes. I felt like I'd done a lousy job for my client. It had been a wild goose chase, all right. But it was coming to closure, and even though we'd defused the Haziri bomb threat in time, I'd left behind a dissatisfied client. Well, I had done my best. What will be, will be. If his daughters are a bunch of vindictive, murdering crooks, I can't let him blame that on me. The apple doesn't fall far from the tree. At least, he still has one semi-honest daughter—the one who got out from under him first.

Under ideal standards which demand maximum efficiency and can be achieved only if everything operates perfectly, I would have located the painting. Currently attainable standards are achieved under efficient operating conditions. I did my personal best, so I guess I met my currently attainable standards. Of course, Henderson did not think so.

Maybe my failing was like a modeling error. Such an error is a deviation from the standard because of a failure to include all relevant variables or because of the inclusion of irrelevant or incorrect variables in the standard setting process.

Hildy stuck her head in the doorway, "Tom wants to know if you need him for anything this morning."

"No. Not right now, thanks."

I got up and felt sluggish. Downstairs, I had a cup of black coffee. The coffee helped some, but not much. Tasted more like gasoline.

I walked several blocks before I stopped by a bus stop, and I climbed on board one that took me to the Village. There was plenty of time, but it was a warm day, and I needed the sun. You can't beat a park bench for that, in the city anyway.

I don't know how long I sat there before Paul Manfred appeared. He was wearing a sleeveless denim jacket over a bare chest and looked like one of the Village locals. He grinned and sat down beside me.

He told me he didn't owe me anything, and I agreed with him. His grin went away, and he looked solemn. "Henderson's getting what he deserved. He stepped on all of us. It was Cora who put the whole idea together. Get him back where it would hurt him the most."

"Why did you bother with the fifty thousand?"

"That was all I wanted. That was enough for me. It was Sandra that brought in Relgado. She needed him. Relgado collected the fifty thousand, and when he handed it over to me he said I was a sap, and that I would owe him big time. I'm not greedy, but when I had the cops looking for me, I went to Sergei for help. I should have known you couldn't trust him for nothing. Instead of handing the painting over to Marilyn, he told me to hide it—in the dump apartment where I was staying on the Lower East Side. If I were caught, they'd pin me for the robbery, and maybe for killing that Walker guy. When things cooled down and they sold the painting, Relgado said he would give me a cut. But when Marilyn didn't get the painting, she went *crazy*, and blew him away. I guess by that time with all the drugs and the murders, she was flippin' out— nobody was going to stop her from gettin' what she wanted."

"*You* have the Turner?"

"Just told ya."

"You mean *you* were the one that locked me in the walk-in?"

"That was *you*? Well, I couldn't let you get the Turner," he said, as if that made sense.

"You miserable ..."

"Well I didn't know it was you."

"Yeah, well maybe you sold it already anyway. You nearly killed me, you ..."

"Look, I told you. I didn't know who it was. The collector Relgado helped them set up to buy the painting doesn't live in the good old USA. He's somewhere in the Balkans, wherever that is. I'll get there. I'll find him. That's why I'm talking to you—you can help me get out of the country, and I'll cut you in for half." He was serious.

"Not me, Jack. You've got fifty thousand dollars. You manage it. Only I don't believe you're going to Eastern Europe. My guess is South America."

"When I sell the painting, I'll send you a postcard."

"Forget it. Don't do me any more favors."

"Look, I didn't steal the painting. Sergei gave it to me."

"Give me a break. You're in possession of stolen property. Maybe Relgado and Henderson received what they deserved. I'm not their judge. But there's blood on that painting—three men. You think you can live with that? You'll never get away with it."

"Why don't you call the police then?"

"I just might," I huffed. "I don't feel like playing the hero today. This is my day off. I'm tired, Manfred. I'm tired of this case. I'm tired of you. I'm tired of the Hendersons. I'm tired of the Hazirian Liberation Army. You do whatever you want. But don't send me any postcards."

Paul Manfred stood up and stretched. "I ain't no two-bit mug anymore. I know that much."

That's what he thinks. I watched him walk off under the arch and down Fifth Avenue. I watched until he was nowhere in sight. The sun was warm on my face. It felt so good. One more call to Steedle, and Manfred was done. Did he really think I'd help him get out of the country? My back ached. I was hungry.

I used my cell phone and called Myra; then I called Steedle. Yes, she would have lunch with me. Why not?

We met in Bryant Park and walked until we found a little French crepe shop. We ordered, and she ate some of her blueberry and cheese crepe. It had white powdered sugar on it. I ate everything in sight. I was famished.

"My father lost two of his daughters, and I've lost Marilyn. It's so unfair."

I was out of talk, so I didn't say anything.

"It's all just a nightmare," she said.

I sipped chocolate-almond flavored cappuccino.

She looked at me. "My father called me. He wants me to come there and stay with him."

Did the old bird still have a soft spot in him after all? "What do you think you will do?" I asked.

She looked faded. Her eyes weren't bright at all. Her grin was a pasty thing to see. At least, I thought so.

"I'm going to live there with him," she said. "I have no place else to go."

I cringed and sipped the last of my cappuccino. What did my grandfather tell me? "Don't spit into the wind. Or something like that."

*   *   *

*Too often senior managers assume that by mechanically eliminating chunks of business or consolidating operations, they will improve the Company's position. In fact, only by designing controllable and highly integrated manufacturing processes—something we call robust—can companies lower overhead permanently and, at the same time, remain viable broadline manufacturers.*

—Mark F. Blaxill and Thomas M. Hout

*Capital budgeting decisions fall into two broad categories—screening decision and preference decisions. Screening decisions relate to whether a proposed project is acceptable—whether it passes a pre-set hurdle. Preference decision, by contrast, relate to selecting from several acceptable alternatives.*

—P.C. Brewer, R.H. Garrinson, and E.W. Norren

# Other Books by D. Larry Crumbley

- *Trap Doors and Trojan Horses: An Auditing Action Adventure*, Carolina Academic Press, 919-489-7486; Fax 919-493-5668. $25.00
- *The Big R: A Forensic Accounting Action Adventure*, Carolina Academic Press, 919-489-7486; Fax 919-493-5668. $25.00
- *Deadly Art Puzzle: Accounting for Murder* (advanced accounting), Carolina Academic Press, 919-469-7486; Fax 919-493-5668. $25.00.
- *Simon the Incredible* (finance), Thomson Corp., 800-355-9983; Fax 800-487-8488; In Europe, Tel: 44-207-0672500 (UK). $24.95
- *The Bottom Line is Betrayal* (general business), Carolina Academic Press, 919-489-7486; Fax 919-493-5668.
- *Accosting the Golden Spire* (basic accounting), Carolina Academic Press, 919-489-7486, Fax 919-493-5668.
- *The Ultimate Rip-off: A Taxing Tale* (taxation), Carolina Academic Press, 919-489-7486, Fax 919-493-5668.
- *Computer Encryptions in Whispering Caves* (accounting information systems), Cengage Corporation, Philip.Krabbe@cengage.com.
- *Chemistry in Whispering Caves* (chemistry), Thomson Corp., 800-355-9983; Fax 800-487-8488; In Europe, Tel: 44-207-0672500 (UK), 1998, $24.95
- *Nonprofit Sleuths: Follow the Money* (governmental accounting), Thomson Corp., 800-355-9983; Fax 800-487-8488; In Europe, Tel: 44-207-0672500 (UK), 1997, $24.95
- *Dangerous Hoops: A Forensic Marketing Action Adventure*, LSU Press, Baton Rouge, 2011.

- Greenspan, *Burmese Caper* (finance), 2 Many Books, 6001 Thoroughbred Ridge, College Station, TX 77845, $25.00.
- Fenton, Jr. and Ziegenfuss, *The Big R: A Forensic Accounting Action Adventure*, Carolina Academic Press, 919-489-7486, Fax 919-493-5668.
- LaGraize and Peters, *Case Study in Forensic and Investigative Accounting*, Wolters Kluwer, 2016, 800-248-3248.
- Fenton, Heitger, Smith, *Forensic and Investigative Accounting*, WoltersKluwer, 800-248-3248.

# Praise for Crumbley's Novel Approach

Called a "cross between Mickey Spillane and Mr. Chips" by the Washington Post, Professor Larry Crumbley (aka Iris Weil Collett) is the author of twelve other widely adopted educational novels. *Business Week* in June 1989, called him a mover and shaker, and said he "aims to lend excitement to the study of debits and credits by couching the stuff in romantic prose." Using forensic accountants as his major characters, a *New Accountant* article called Crumbley the Mark Twain of the accounting profession.

Crumbley's goal is to spice up ho-hum subjects to make students think that the accounting profession is much better than the stereotype image they have. Think CSI. According to the *Wall Street Journal*, his novels prove the phrase "suspenseful accounting is not necessarily an oxymoron."

*Fortune,* June 29, 1991, quoted Crumbley: "to be a good accountant, you have to be a good detective" and called his latest novel an "instructional thriller." Crumbley appeared on the front cover of the December 1988 issue of *Management Accounting* as a bespectacled Mickey Spillane. Kathy Williams, author of "The Case of the Purloined Pagoda" said to "move over Arthur Hailey." *WG&L Accounting News* compared Crumbley to Indiana Jones. The fedora-donned, trench coat Crumbley could be the John D. MacDonald in the accounting arena with thirteen novels under his belt.

Allow your students to have fun while they learn managerial accounting under the scenario principle. Don't spoon feed your students, but entertain them while you teach.